CW00485533

Strong Spirit, Weak Heart

By

William Tell

Published in 2012 by FeedARead.com Publishing – Arts Council funded

Copyright © William Tell

The author or authors assert their moral right under the Copyright, Designs and Patents Act, 1988, to be identified as the author or authors of this work.

All Rights reserved. No part of this publication may be reproduced, copied, stored in a retrieval system, or transmitted, in any form or by any means, without the prior written consent of the copyright holder, nor be otherwise circulated in any form of binding or cover other than that in which it is published and without a similar condition being imposed on the subsequent purchaser.

A CIP catalogue record for this title is available from the British Library.

INTRODUCTION

Strong Spirit, Weak Heart.

A story of hope and survival against the odds that challenged the mind, body and spirit. This book links seamlessly with **Downing Street Species** and presents a unique story of life and near death challenges for William. From poor roots to high places it describes unbelievable but true life episodes of psychic mystery witnessed by many. It describes survival against the odds, his psychic and healing abilities, which amazed him as much as the many people it touched. His message is that we all have a life mission for the greater good and our actions as a ripple effect can make a positive difference, touching many both near and afar.

William's older brother drowned in a canal before he and his twin brother Tom were born. William was destined to save four people from drowning in four separate events in his lifetime. He prepared for and survived his first battle against the odds on a lucky Friday 13th 1992 in the Lake District. William went on to survive a further eight more life threatening events and associated challenges over the next 20 years.

For a Channel 4 TV production (Psychic Detectives) he got into the mind of mass murderer GP Dr Harold Shipman. He was later to visualise and describe much of the case evidence material in the tragic murder of schoolgirl Milly Dowler. Key information he documented years before the police made it public. For others he was to see in his minds eye their possessions, birth dates, health secrets, body scars, pain points and silent matters of the heart and soul. In one event he saw blood on the wrists before he

3

entered a small room and found that very scene. He was to read the mind of a clairvoyant and know her pain the night before they met as he lay in bed contemplating his first reading with her. Healing support to others often produced real benefits to the sufferers much to his and their surprise.

He foresaw the MP expense scandal some eight years before the event. On expenses, the economy and Iraq Downing Street was not for turning. Sir Richard Branson, like William had a strategy to avoid war but Blair took the military path with Bush. William foresaw the TV documentary title featuring the Prime Minister's wife and the rainbow that appeared at the leaving of office for Tony Blair before those events became public. All the facts and psychic type events presented can be validated by witnesses and related documents.

ACKNOWLEDGEMENTS

With gratitude and love to my mother, father and other such selfless people in the community of life who provided the basis of what politics should be about. That is to selflessly work towards making a positive difference in the lives of others. With thanks and much love and appreciation to my wife, daughters, son, family and friends, who are much loved and supported me in so many ways over the years. My love will last as long as the stars shine bright in the dark sky above.

Many thanks also to the medical staff and teams who saved my life so many times over the years and provided so many more chapters in my life since the morning of the Friday 13th November 1992 when my heart stopped. Reborn with a spirit strengthened for the years to follow. Thanks also for those who provided much support in producing this book.

THE AUTHOR

William has always believed that life is about working towards making a positive difference in the lives of others. That belief has been with him since an early age. Recognising that we all have strengths, weaknesses and human frailties he believes that adding value to other people's lives is a key goal worth working for.

William enjoyed a loving, caring working class family childhood close to the docklands in Liverpool, UK and lived in a small council house. This was at times a home also to budgerigars, a large owl, hens, various reptiles and pets. A nocturnal home also to armies of cockroaches, which invaded the ground floor rooms when the lights were turned off at night. William is an identical twin, one of the seven children in the family. His mother toiled in local factories or cleaned pub toilets and bars to support the family. His dad hurt his spine whilst working as a dock labourer and suffered both the disability and the financial consequences. However there was always food to eat, second hand clothing mostly to wear and cramped caravan holidays by the seaside when it was affordable. From Liverpool dockland home to dining on a millionaires yacht in Hong Kong harbour, supping beer with a Government Minister in Parliament and being interviewed by the BBC whilst in 10 Downing Street William experienced a life of rainbow and storm-cloud contrasts.

William is a psychic with some healing abilities who has had many unexplained insights since a near death experience. Insights and predictions into future events, into the lives of others were witnessed by many credible people like a senior figure in a Government Ministry, Solicitors, Doctors, Nurses, College Tutor and many others. From those poor roots he progressed from apprentice engineer to management consultancy and adviser to politicians, the public, private and not for profit sectors. His career role took him to Downing Street, UK/European Parliament, China and across the UK. He provided advice and support to individuals, business start-ups, PLCs, the NHS, national and local companies, charities and a major political party. He co-founded The Democracy Trust in 2000. William is married with five children and four grandchildren.

LIST OF CHAPTERS:

1

THE ANGEL ABOVE

Satisfaction in her soul, warmed by her endeavours she gazed at his face beneath her. Conscious of his steady heart but unaware of the hidden spirit immersed within his resting body. Her knees now released from his waist, as an act of love, without love, on the bed of passion. A strange frenzy of emotions and spent force unique in a fleeting union. Like strangers whose eyes met, hearts raced, thoughts spinning. Touched by soul contact in one brief moment never to be repeated. Contact ended abruptly, doors slamming but new paths taken as fate directs them apart. Bonded briefly for eternity but separated that day to unknown destinies in life's mission. She was silent now, dressed warm in the uniform of a nurse, her forehead tinged with beads of sweat. She hesitated before removing her hands and body from his drained form.

Satisfied with the result of her labours, her energy all but expended during the frantic moments now discharged. For both, a life-charging outcome glimpsed as snapshots in lenses of the minds eye for years to follow. For him a heart-break beyond repair, a spirit challenged. For her, intense and satisfying in both a professional and personal way, feeding the senses of mind, body and soul. Forever an unforgotten experience, etched perhaps as a sentence or two in a chapter in the book of her memories. Another episode for him in his life journey, now the start-point of a story yet to relate. Fact or fiction, fantasy or reality, how many would believe what came before, what followed afterwards and what was yet to come.

The pleasure for her was real, yet unspoken as she broke the special bond and detached herself from her achievement on the bed. The bed of witness to his helplessness, his blissful detachment from the frantic passion before. The passion of survival to again seek love, to live for others and pass time with the years. His heart-ache new and life-lasting, with the battle for the heart hard won but more battles ahead. She was the saviour of his heart but not of his soul. For him and others to follow, her gift used once more to etch in stone another step in the stairwell of her life's mission. Looking to heaven his new life began by lifting his head from the pillow, to gaze on the angel above. One of many, here evermore amongst us and in places beyond our dreams. Somewhere over or even part of the rainbow of life perhaps.

Outstretched on the bed his eyes flickered, released from a hypnotic sleep counted perhaps in seconds, minutes or, as eternity with infinite distance travelled. A forgotten episode he would always wonder. A serene journey from this place to another for a brief reunion with the source of love and place of loved ones. Spiritual travel, blissful even, without pain, without the ticking of the clock or the turning of the screw. All emotions, sights, senses, sounds erased from his mortal memory. Turned away from a much better place bathed in light to return to this world. To be challenged by dark forces, earthly demands, tugging, tearing in many, many directions. Again to face shaded vistas, evil forces and life's constant struggle. Balanced however in many ways by goodness, the beauty, the hopes, dreams and above all the love in this world.

Shocked in different ways he found around him what seemed a human wall, an audience of many gathered at the bedside. Some dressed in the garb of white purity, others in uniforms of colour, all participants and witnesses to a seed sown that morning starting a new life. A new life for him and for others as yet unknown, untouched by his presence, his strengths and many weaknesses. On awakening as re-born he thought of his loved ones, his wife in particular and quickly judged the situation before him. Leaving the tunnel of white light and answers now erased he decided short reflection with an immediate response was needed. Time was of the essence with a threat manifested evermore.

He removed the oxygen mask from his face and said quietly to those around him *I don't want to sound dramatic – but if anything happens to me, tell my wife I love her very much.* The earthly angel above and life giver was to tell loved ones later that tears clouded her eyes with those words. Those words spoken, whilst looking to a window framing the low hills. A vista dotted with moving white life forms, like snow, but not snow in the district of lakes and much beauty. Mountains in the distance with peaks to climb also in life matters over future years. The year was 1992 and the day was Friday, November 13th. The time was 8.20 in the morning.

A day shrouded with superstition, painted as a dark number and dealer of bad luck in the annals of folklore and tales handed down. For him a new start, which found him savouring life nervously in the years to come. But for him a day he had prepared for, which destiny decreed. A day that was also his mother's birthday, which made it a special day and as it turned out one hell of a lucky day so close to heaven. He was a young, strong 44 year old now helpless to the unfolding and surreal situation that cast a haze around him. A thirteenth day of Friday but luck and strange powers had sought him out amongst the many. Fate served him well and directed him on the step of his own stairwell to destiny. I was the man on the bed experiencing a massive heart attack/cardiac arrest in hospital that special morning, that special day with an angel above.

A day to remember. Frightening with life-lasting effects but strangely with unforeseen benefits yet to experience. An ironic twist to the fantasy of many men to share a bed with a young lady in nurse uniform. To have a woman on top, in control on a bed would have a different meaning from that point on, as it transpired not a position or scenario to be sought in the future. The electric shock defibrillator had done the trick and re-started my heart, albeit without the pads designed to protect the skin. Both pads had gone astray and the slightly burnt chest was a small price to pay from the professionals giving back my life.

The new start was made safe by the skilled team and wonderful woman pumping my chest, keeping me alive with God's help. I was to find out some years later that only half the defibrillator shocked heart attack patients survive such treatment and only a third leave hospital alive. One third of my heart was destroyed that day never to recover. However Friday 13th was indeed a lucky day in my life's journey. Weak heart but a stronger spirit yet to manifest. I started on a new mortal trail of unique experiences, albeit with help from other untouchable forces, unseen within me or around me. I was to meet and sought to influence three men, Blair, Brown and Cameron who became Prime Ministers. I spoke to many MPs, Ministers and Shadow Ministers, was also *email friend* to Cherie Blair in my search for a democracy of common good aims based on sensible politics. In search of a system putting people first before party politics or personalities. I met many household names and celebrities from TV and beyond including Miss World, *I'am a celebrity* Jungle contestants Esther Rantzen, Christine Hamilton and husband ex MP Neil, an X Factor winner/singer.

On ex-Boxer Chris Eubank I did an impromptu psychic reading on in a bar in Alderley Edge. Ex-UK Ambassador to the USA Sir Christopher Meyer, John Culshaw, impressionist and comedian were all fascinating people, who added flavour and interest to my new start in life.

It was a life of storm and rainbow like contrasts with bright auras, solar in origin to experience. A light force emerging from within and around and long days and even darker nights to endure. Many challenges of the physical and the heart arose. Never ending it seemed but lightened by psychic mysteries appearing briefly like shooting stars witnessed by many. My body used as a conduit for unspoken words for reasons unknown. I was told later that all mankind were spirits on earth and that we did not suddenly move on to become spirits as we already exist in that form. Spirits packaged as human vessels. Living souls with inherent freedom of purpose and action influenced by mind, body, fellow mankind, wonders of earth and competing forces. Here, as we all are in a galaxy for just a blink of time, as a flash of lightening, a cloud burst, a twinkle in the sunset, a rainbow in passing. Our lifetime measured by eternity before, beyond and by infinity of space and dimension encircling us all.

As with all spirits on earth I had mountains to surmount, desolate valleys to travel and places to gain meaning from. Alive to walk a beautiful world framed with special moments to treasure, too vivid to capture fully on canvas or screen. Paths were to be followed leading to insurmountable heights, wasted journeys. Yet so often compensated by fruitful travel, faithful companions, small steps on walls embedded in the other side of the world as seen from space. Re-born, yet much, much weaker than before my life ebbed and flowed with destiny's force. A life mission ahead implanted as a secret companion since before birth. My life always considered as a mission for something greatly significant and good to achieve, but not really certain what that something was. Perhaps everyone felt that way I thought. I should ask that question of others.

As a grain of sand in vast oceans of swirling sand, yet with substance, of potential as we all to create a pearl within a life shell of great value. Offering appeal and worth to others if the shifting currents and God did so decree. I went on to develop the gift described as psychic ability by some, demonstrated by seeing from within and knowing what I shouldn't have knowledge of. Mediumistic and a healing support ability used with some people I met was also part of my life gifts. Gifts experienced by many credible people. Strange experiences with life situations of others, presented in intuitive thoughts. Uncannily originating from an unknown place. Hidden facts revealed within me as snapshots of stranger's lives, validated by the recipients as accurate incursions into life events. My various proposals passed on to Tony Blair via Cherie, was somewhat prophetic prior to the Iraq invasion and the legacy of Blair's rush to war was to come back to haunt him. Nelson Mandela, with Sir Richard Branson whose initiative was approved by United Nations, Koffi Annan were also on the same wavelength but the bombs started falling before peace was waged. How could I foresee the MP expense scandal some eight years before in 2001 when only 26 out of 659 MPs responded to my written standard for selfless politics ?.

How did I know the name of the BBC documentary – *The Real Cherie* when I emailed Cherie Blair at Downing Street and how did I know a rainbow would be of significance to the Blairs when they were making their goodbyes to the people ?. How in a logical world based on scientific evidence could I know instantly the hidden medical conditions of two strangers when they walked in a room and sat in my company ? Both looked at each other with incredulity when I relayed inner knowledge of their frailties. They confirmed the message delivered as thoughts to me was correct and could not comprehend how I knew. I could not comprehend how I knew. For others before that day and following years I was to see in my minds eye their possessions, birth dates, health secrets, body scars, pain points and silent matters of the heart and soul. In one event I was to see blood on the wrists before I entered a small room and found that very scene.

I was to read the mind of a clairvoyant and know her pain the night before we met as I lay in bed contemplating my first reading with her. I was to describe the type of car, colour of car, white van and specific relevant factors connected with a terrible abduction and murder of beautiful teenage girl, Milly Dowler some 230 miles away before detectives released those details to the media many years later. A Channel 4 production company (Cactus) who filmed me were posted a copy of my written analysis following the murder but took it no further as did the police when I contacted them. In contrast, the psychic insights in some cases seemed crazy, laughable and embarrassing even – how did I know that the highly placed civil servant had not one but two yellow toy ducks in his bath when bathing ? – For the civil servant serving in an edifice of power in Whitehall, a toy legacy from childhood unknown to the world except for the man's wife and young children. How did I know a small mouse was silently exploring a darkened room before I opened the door to that room ?. How did I know family issues and city of travel to a far place for the lady behind the voice on the telephone 210 miles away ?. Chillingly I was to enter the mind of the mass murderer doctor Harold Shipman GP, feel nausea and much later discover he had killed my namesake.

As an identical twin I took on a different life's purpose than my twin brother, feeling I was born for a reason wrapped in the moon shadow of destiny with episodes of my life written before birth. As the younger of the two by twenty minutes we twins, Thomas and

William were born in Liverpool at Walton Hospital, 1 – 9 – 48 of the year 1,9,48. I was born at 19.00 hrs. A numerologist may look closely at the numbers and ponder about the unique sequence of birth-date, time of birth etc, which d.o.b. number pattern spells out the year numbers with it. Our family lived close to the banks of the River Mersey in Liverpool and were poor but proud sons and daughters of the tribe from the pool, known as *Liverpudlians* or *Scousers*. We lived a short bus ride away from Cherie Booth/Blair later to become a world stage figure and our paths periodically crossed years later both by email dialogue and face to face chats.

When she lived in 10 Downing Street over the years I offered words of advice, (as you would to the alleged *12th most powerful woman in the world)* for her to pass on to the Prime Minister. Advice of course not taken but history was to prove the lowly one (me) and others right regarding the invasion to topple the dictator and other matters of leadership, political standards and Tony Blair's legacy. Cherie's local beach in Crosby as a youngster was also our beach to visit. As children we would sit by the concrete pill box fortifications left over from the war years devouring a poor family's picnic of tap water in lemonade bottles with egg sandwiches. We called sandwiches *butties*. The Mersey river mud - pollution and all was used as sun tan cream on hot summer days and we would fish for crabs in the River Mersey at Bootle docks.

We twins were birth sign Virgo's. The family story was that we were to be christened Peter and Paul but Dad got sidetracked to the pub, drank heavily with relatives and ended up registering our name as William and Thomas. Later known to the family and close friends as Billy and Tommy. Both Perfectionists by birth sign but not perfect in any way. Sadly for our family some weeks before our birth an elder brother named George had drowned in the dark waters of a nearby canal aged ten. George's mother, our mother known in the family as Mam (Sarah) then went on to give birth to me, (as events unfolded, reincarnation some were to say) and my identical twin. Mam was to thank God for having a second baby now that George was lost to this world. One twin born was seen by Mam, Dad and others to replace George whose short lived path to a better place touched all their lives. Life then unfolded for me the younger twin with special tasks ahead and challenges to overcome. Destiny intervened in my life journey, which led me many years later to save the lives of four people from drowning on four separate occasions. Was it coincidence, fate or destiny ?. Who on earth could with total confidence and conviction could answer that question ?.

By being in the right places at the right times I had made my personal mark on life but how strange that I, the poor swimmer was placed by the waters edge on hand to prevent further tragedies. On hand strangely to save one child in the same stretch of canal where my elder brother drowned. Another boy who fell off the cliffside into the sea. The third person being a girlfriend swept away by a fast current in a river in the south of France. The fourth person being my own toddler daughter Lucy who slipped under the water unnoticed by others in a crowded swimming pool. I went in after her fully clothed but she was unperturbed and probably thought her dad was mad. No hero as such but why was it that I was to probably prevent death for others and later on survive death myself on eight or so occasions also ?. In 2012 my wife and I were near a sea-wall in a sea-side resort in North West England and I spotted two very young girls struggling along the sloping wall with the sea lapping at their feet and on the wrong side of the safety railings. One slip and they could have drowned in the waves below. I stopped a passing police car and we got them to safety. Again why was I there at the right time to contribute to their safety ?. One day I will, I believe be provided with the answers again, which as yet are not revealed to us.

Growing to manhood I never connected the potential drownings I had prevented in any way as a link with George's death. One day though my much loved Aunt Marie, who was near death in hospital suggested I may have been born a life with that special purpose. Whatever the reasons, of destiny or coincidence, life had gained greater value with the four saved and for that I thanked God. More of a sinner than saintly in my life's journey, a poet when inspired, with a love of words and reading but a user of foul language not to be too proud of when provoked.

Well I suppose TV Chef celebrities and *Big Brother* type shows have set the scene but my bad language failings pale into insignificance by comparison. My path would take me through two numbered doors of Downing Street and to stagger out somewhat drunk from one of those doors. Binge drinking at the heart of power, arranged by the powerful lawmakers. Not however drunk on power but drunk with the plentiful wine supplied by business sponsors. Perhaps the sponsors had good reasons for providing the booze.

Later on I would politely intrude into Government policies - world events even as predicted by she my clairvoyant soothsayer with the unseen pains. I was later invited to contribute to a Channel 4 TV Richard & Judy show with a Danny Wallace as producer researching psychic phenomena. I experienced overpowering nausea looking into the mind of a mass murderer (of alleged hundreds) who left this world by suicide to avoid justice. I was to find out only months later that the murderer, named Harold Shipman had most likely murdered a man of my own identical name, rare as my name was in this country. To see my own name on the list of probable victims and talk to the victim's family was a uniquely unnerving experience.

Prior to 1992 and for reasons unknown I felt a dice with death was written into my life plot before I existed. Some strange instinct or premonition made me prepare for such a day. I always felt I had a special purpose in life and a role to play that was nagging me and would not let go until fulfilled. I had a strange feeling for many, many years that I would face death at an early age. Although failing on many occasions to be a good person I always believed that we were here on this planet of beauty and badlands to be selfless and make a positive difference to the lives of others. I believed we were here to be judged by a greater force and that our main purpose was to be tested in our lifetime, as short or as long as it may be. Without any symptoms and for financial reasons etc some months before Friday 13th I had a full medical screening and was declared fit and healthy by a doctor. With low cholesterol, a slim build, non-smoker I was considered by the experts as a fine specimen and sent on my way with a message to carry on with my reasonably healthy life-style. However sometime before I had followed my inner voice and insured myself to the limit for a full range of medical and critical illness insurances. You name it, everything was insured including car hire purchase and everything else under the sun. Like Russian roulette based on premonition, some inner instinct, insider information even I had placed a special bet against a future episode of a critical life threatening illness I might face one day. The bet was based on no previous symptoms as I was declared fit by health screening and my unscientific gut feeling, premonition or whatever would provide me with funds to pay the bills when it was needed most. Some gamble !.

A few days before my brush with death I had a letter from my bank manager listing my families various accounts, overdrafts and loans in excess of five figures and implying that the bank might pull the financial rug if no action was taken. As the main provider for bringing up children meant that providing for a family of six, our home and two business ventures money was always tight and finances extremely overstretched. I wrote back to the bank saying that our outgoings were high because of costly monthly premiums to insurance companies to protect the family against medical/income disaster. This fact was absolutely true but as with many banking representatives they failed to understand the reality of living and cash flow for some families and small businesses. Thank goodness my instinct was correct and I was ahead of him in financial safeguards for the home and family, albeit overstretched in paying those insurances.

We had also over-extended with our limited finances to buy a nice house with a swimming pool for the children and us to use. Running a new business from scratch and travelling the length and breadth of the country to meet the bills was taking its toll in many ways. Shortly before my heart attack whilst stuck in a traffic jam I read a letter from our bank manager about our serious financial situation. Later that morning, probably due to immense fatigue due to the heart malfunction and/or with a dangerous lack of concentration I wrote the car off in a traffic accident. I luckily survived and no one else was injured in the process. After my heart attack my bank manager later went on to describe my traumatic brush with death as *a blessing in disguise* in a letter to me some weeks after my cardiac arrest. For that and other reasons, he was in my mind either an idiot, devoid of sensitivity or a man of great perception. Some people do have the best of intentions though. Whilst recovering at home a week or so after my heart attack one dear neighbour brought my wife a video for me to watch. The film was called *flatliner*, which involved young people dicing with their lives by inducing death and then recovering with a heart start electric defibrillator. Needless to say I was chilled by the film title and didn't dare watch the video. The neighbour oblivious to the trauma I had undergone had good intentions (or maybe was just taking the piss as they say) but unwisely chosen a film of potential to scare the hell out of me and even cause me cardiac arrest and flat-line. Maybe it was a devilish plot by my wife to get hold of the life insurance monies !.

With my premonition or whatever it was I had also had written a will that summer, wrote a note of farewell and had placed a card in my wallet listing all the contact numbers and names in my family to contact. *In the event of me falling ill*, was the first line on that card, which I passed over to someone when my heart attack started. I had no previous diagnosis or symptoms to point to impending heart failure. They say telepathy – especially with twins is documented and in our case this was true. On that fateful Friday my twin had a premonition some 250 miles away that something was amiss and he dropped everything and he was already on the road to travel north when my near death episode was unfolding. I was a business advisor working away from home in Kendal in the Lake District as part of a team managing the national reorganisation of a Plc Insurance company. The night before I enjoyed a night out at bars and discos in the town of Kendal with my team colleagues. It was a hell of a night and I returned to the public house hotel more drunk than sober to awake with a hangover competing with my heart attack and as it turned out embarking on a new chapter in a my life. I normally slept without pyjamas but because of the cold hotel room I had bought and worn pyjamas that night.

I awoke at about 7-45am with a terrific hangover and strange rushing noises in my head. Like waves crashing on the shorelines of my skull. I felt a heavy pressure on my chest and had trouble breathing. With no phone in my annex room, nor mobile phone then, I managed to stagger out of bed (thankfully not naked) to the hotel reception. I asked the manager to phone for an ambulance and requested he use the card held in my wallet with contact names to urgently contact my family. I lay outstretched and shivering on a cold bench in the bar of the hotel, which reeked of spilt ale and cigarette smoke whilst waiting anxiously for the ambulance. The hotel manager looked frightened to death. Perhaps he didn't like the thought of giving me mouth to mouth resuscitation as I hadn't had time to clean my teeth and maybe smelt of booze from the previous night.

The paramedics arrived, placed me in the ambulance, gave me an aspirin and an ECG. I knew I was having a heart attack and they quickly confirmed it. Luckily for me, so vulnerable in the middle of the Lake District there was a brand new purpose built cardiac unit in a brilliant hospital three minutes drive away. They took me by the ambulance to accident & emergency department. I was fast tracked to a state of the art (and heart) coronary care unit and ECG monitored bed. I was rapidly given a life saving blood-thinning drug called *Streptokinase*. The doctors told me later that within half an hour of admission my ECG trace started going haywire as my heart failed and that's when the *crash* resuscitation team raced to my bed and thankfully saved my life. The nurse angel I saw straddling my body on the bed when I returned to the world was witness to the start of my new life as well as being part of the team of brilliant people who saved me that day. When my wife and family came they were told I was seriously ill and the next few days were crucial. I was later to learn from a heart specialist that nearly a third of my heart had died that day and I had suffered something called left ventricular dysfunction resulting from the cardiac arrest. This was to prove a life lasting condition.

Weak heart was inflicted that day with the spirit faced by an ongoing battle to gather strength over the years and many challenges to follow. I was to spend ten days in that hospital looking out to the hills counting the sheep as they munched and defecated their way over the landscape. The shock of the heart failure hit me that first day when my first visitor arrived. His name was Mike and he was a senior manager with the company I was working with. The tears flooded my eyes when Mike was kind to me, perhaps heightened by the morphine I was on. He told me he could understand my feelings as shock often follows trauma. He was witness to the Bradford football ground fire when many people died or were badly burnt he told me. He said he had experienced first hand the trauma and the delayed shock after the disaster and had some understanding of how shock manifests itself. He was brilliant and offered his personal support and books for me to read. His Plc company kindly went on to house my wife in a local hotel for the hospital stay duration of ten days but stopped my consultancy earnings from the day before the heart attack. For twelve months I was working around the clock before my hospitalisation and travelling all over the country with stressful deadlines to meet. In 1992 the compensation culture was not prevalent but perhaps I had a good case for stress compensation, which was never considered by me. I had other things on my mind of course.

After a few days I was moved to an ordinary ward and slowly started to recover. A nervous wreck then and for some time to come, afraid to close my eyes in case I didn't wake up in the morning. For years afterwards I nearly panicked when an ambulance went by with siren blaring. I wrote a *just in case* goodbye letter to everyone to be followed by a few more just in case farewell notes over the years to my loved ones. Afraid then of even indigestion and small twinges in my chest. Thinking they were the start of a heart attack, which would finish me before my life mission was complete. Some days in Kendal Hospital produced lighter moments though. A man on the ward for tests and in-patient observation had strangely lost his voice and kept us all amused with attempts at sign language and written notes to people. However he forgot his charade and search for sympathy one evening and said *good night* to a ward cleaner. He wandered off mumbling *dear, dear* to himself and was promptly discharged after his miraculous recovery. God moves in mysterious ways.

My spirit started on its trail of revival when my very attractive wife took me for my first shower on the ward after day five of ward recovery. My survival and latent amorous instincts engaged battle with my overriding fear of expiring in that shower and my wife being left to deal with the guilt. Having people say to her that *he died content with a smile on his face* would be of no comfort to her or the family. I cannot reveal which life force won but can only say a strength of will battle took place in the shower room. She was a nervous wreck but I wanted to feel human again after sharing a ward with the frail and elderly. Many visitors and relatives came to visit me in hospital including my Mam who had such a shocking surprise on her birthday that November 13th. My twin brother told me he had some foreboding instinct that day and drove up towards Liverpool, which was uncanny but enabled him to collect my mother and make arrangements for my family. His own mortality was probably in question in his mind that black Friday as he was of course genetically identical to me. However if he was nervous he never showed it or discussed his fears with me.

On the final Sunday in hospital I attended the hospital church service as the only man amongst two-dozen females and thanked God for my survival. I left hospital after about ten days and was driven home in a most anxious state after leaving the hospital cocoon of safety with security and life-savers on call 24/7. I was to face eight or more life threatening encounters and experience major surgery, around thirty operations or invasive procedures over the following years. I was to experience periodic exhaustion, severe pain, recurrent challenges to my health - twice including great blood loss, arduous surgery, hospital acquired infection causing severe knock on effects including me losing a stone in weight and worse. My main artery in my heart blocked up eight times over those years. I also had in the scheme of things medically a not so scary skin cancer diagnosis related operation. This was all during my efforts as a lowly mortal to influence decision makers and make the world a better place. God had set some challenges and I had to keep on going. Medically it was one step forward, three steps back. However in my life's journey I was to count myself lucky and my heart went out to those children and adults I was yet to meet or see who had greater physical challenges than I.

On my life's journey so many coincidences have sprinkled that pathway that I honestly believe they are not coincidences. They happen for a reason. Me being at hand by the waters edge on 4 separate occasions when 4 people nearly drowned has no logical answer to it. So called coincidences are somehow road signs along the way and should not be ignored or discounted as they are aspects of all our missions in life. For example my twin brother has two lovely daughters named Jo and Lesley, whom I consider as my own much loved daughters. Jo has definitely psychic and healing abilities and we compare notes sometimes on life. I had just got off the phone to her after telling her about finishing getting my books ready as ebooks and titles/author name etc and was driving home from my local pub after a quick beer. The car radio was on BBC Radio 4 classical when I turned it on. The music blasting out less than 5 minutes after discussing the William Tell launch aspirations was indeed the William Tell overture. An inspiring musical piece I had never heard for over thirty years. Jo was amazed as I was. Coincidences should be vital elements to be considered as bookmarks or pointers within the chapters of our books of living.

For me a stronger spirit was later to emerge and do battle but lose as well as win some of those battles as events played out on the journey ahead. My psychic and healing gifts were to develop as time went by. I was satisfied however that as a pebble into a still pond the ripple effect of my new life produced more positives for loved ones and others. For that I was grateful for the borrowed time afforded me.

2
EARLY YEARS

Until I was 27 I lived with my family in council houses in Bootle, near Liverpool not far from the docks. The first of the two council house homes was at 223 King Avenue, Bootle. It was a small three bed-roomed house and had just about escaped the German blitz during the war years. The story in family folklore was that a German incendiary bomb went through the roof of the neighbours house and my Dad (named John) and neighbour entered the loft after returning from the pub. Somewhat drunk they had trouble putting the fire out and it was said they both had to pee on the fire, which did the trick. A risky business considering the fresh alcohol in their breath and urine.

I had older brothers, Jimmy, John and my twin Tommy who was 20 minutes older than me. Also George the elder brother who had sadly drowned in the local Leeds to Liverpool canal in Bootle before we were born. Jean was our elder sister and Richard my younger brother. Jean had a series of relationships, which resulted in four children from four fathers, each with healthy mixed race genes. One of her children, Lorraine lived with us most of the years of our childhood and the other children periodically stayed at home with us. Lorraine was our niece but to us was our sister and a seamless part of the family. Lorraine called my parents Mam and Dad, her real Mum she called Jean. She eventually met her real father in America when she was much older. He was sadly to die a few years after they met. My sister Jean died suddenly after a short illness in 2010 after being treated for arthritis, which actually turned out to be terminal cancer.

We were in the main a happy but poor family. Mam, whose name was Sarah came from Buckingham Street, just off Scotland Road in Liverpool. We used to visit our Grandmother there who was some time back a money-lender. Gran's husband was a hero soldier of the first world war with a medal to prove it. Unfortunately he had died before we were born. He was a good looking guy based on his photograph in soldiers uniform. What hell he went through in the killing fields, mud and slaughter of trench warfare we will never know. Mam kept our house in Bootle clean and tidy although it was infested with cockroaches. A house they say having been built on an old rubbish landfill site. Each morning we would have to turn our shoes upside down to check for cockroaches dozing in the warmth of the shoes. Some nights when going downstairs for a drink of water after switching the light on it revealed what seemed like thousands of new born cockroaches scattering in panic to dark places as a black and brown wave rippling over the floor.

We had an outside toilet, (called the *lav*) clean but freezing in the winter months and with plenty of toilet paper in the form of the Liverpool Echo newspaper cut up into convenient squares. Some scousers would joke that the local news was *crap*. However quiet moments in the outside toilet with reading material started off a love of reading and provided a quiet retreat from the noisy household. Primitive as it sounds it was the norm in the neighbourhood in the fifties to also have a bucket at the top of the stairs for the family to use during the cold nights. A ritual akin to a jailed prisoners *slopping out* duty in the morning before breakfast.

Accidents did sometimes happen however going down the stairs with the full bucket, especially following a night of heavy drinking in the pub by my Dad or brothers. For some reason as custom and practice, we also used outstretched pages of the broadsheet Liverpool Echo as a blind across the front room window at night. Without drawing the curtains the paper was hooked onto the middle window catch as a screen. It was a cheap way of keeping prying eyes out and was considered the norm in the street. Mam's way of using the Echo in the lounge and the toilet was recycling at its finest although hard on the bottom and frustrating if the window-blind newsprint was hung upside down so we couldn't read it. In those days newspapers were also used as outer wrappers by the fish and chip shop.

Mam was the centre of the family, the beating heart and mind of our family unit with Dad as the main provider. He was the laid back soul of the household and the fixer of the broken, the teller of jokes and drinker of pints with his boys in the local Higson's brewery Linacre pub in Bootle. He would often break into song and he was known to stand on his head in the pub just for a laugh. Mam and Dad were both lovely people, givers rather than takers, so generous and loved by all. In those days emotions were never properly demonstrated after the toddler hugs and cuddles stage.

We never kissed or said we loved you. It was not what our family did but we all did love each other with words unspoken and deeds carried out. We were close knit and family was indeed King in King Avenue and beyond. With hardly a front garden we had a small garden in the back leading onto a square of green, which was eventually built on and called by the visionaries in Bootle Council - Stone Square. I was later to have the first kiss of my life with the girl next door – Carol Hoey, with us both standing in a trench dug for a house foundation on the Square. Innocent days to be followed by a womanising career spanning twenty years or more with many women to share in life's pleasures or otherwise. My excuse was I, as a Virgo was searching for the perfect woman. Although some men think they are perfect I was to meet that contender for the title of *Gods gift to women* and travel to the great-wall of China with him. That is another story.

Back home at 223 we had a shed in the garden and the lads had a club there started by my elder brother Jimmy. In his wisdom Jimmy decided that to become a member of the shed club the initiation ceremony was the removal of the light bulb, the licking/wetting of a finger and sticking of the finger into the light socket. Jimmy would flick the light switch for a second or so and if you removed your finger you were a coward and couldn't join the club. I and other unsuspecting friends all became members to our delight and ignorant recklessness. Blackened fingertips like cajun chicken to be hidden or explained away to our parents.

Amazingly we all survived and I was of course to experience more electric of the life saving sort in my body some 30 years in the future.

Our house was unheated except for a coal fire in the front room, which also heated the hot water tank. In winter it was freezing in the bedrooms in particular with ice on the windows and frosty breath when we breathed out. Central heating in those days at home was a dream light years away. Strangely enough though that some fifty or so years later wood burning stoves are becoming more popular as people get concerned about energy supply cost and continuity when countries like the Russians have such a stranglehold on European gas supplies.

My elder brother John told us that during one severe winter they resorted to burning old coats to keep the room warm and water hot when the coal ran out. Old army overcoats covered a double bed I shared with my twin and most of the other beds in the house. My memories of old army blankets on the bed recall that they were *as rough as a bears ass* - as described by some. Luckily for us they didn't have bullet holes or blood stains in them as a reminder of their war service. In bed I was separated from twin Tommy with a home made long pillow running down the centre of the bed. The pillow was called *humpty dumpty* and requested by us to keep our boyish bottoms from touching when we were in bed reading or asleep. Reading by torch under the sheets was a favourite pastime when Mam had turned the lights out. Jimmy slept in a single bed in the corner of the room with the luxury of private air space around him.

We were all naughty and getting into scrapes, some more serious than others. Jimmy over the years had managed to acquire a machine gun (eg a sten gun), a samurai sword, an air pistol and a rifle. Nobody was harmed in the process as far as I recall. I do remember him taking a pot-shot at the bottom of a neighbour's son with what I thought was an air pistol – Jimmy swears that it was only a catapult. The guy was hit on his bottom and did not suffer any lasting damage and is still unaware of the identity of the sniper in the bedroom. above.

As kids we were to make all sorts of primitive weapons from scrap materials and tree branches. We made quite powerful and potentially lethal bows and arrows with quivers tipped with battered tin can parts as arrowheads and hen feathers as flights for the arrows. In waste ground behind the houses we would practice with the weapons, which included large spears made in a similar fashion launched with a sling-shot device. Brick fights would ensue with gangs of other children invading our territory and pieces of brick, sharp shards of slate and large pebbles flung across from group to group. Apart from some bruising and scrapes we were lucky not to maim or kill some future brain surgeon, rocket scientist or mad politician.

On that field we were to dig underground tunnels, risk death by cave-in and search for buried treasure, historic finds and bodies. In the winter we would make igloos from the snow and ice and build ice paths down the centre of our road by constant sliding over the icy ground in our boots. Cold water poured over the slide at night froze overnight to extend our winter sports. Snowball fights were enjoyed well into the evenings against the gas lamps in the street. Street games called *tick* or *lalioa* were played in the innocence of our youth before TV, social media and technology had taken hold of the nation and sculptured our values and ambitions. Tying a rope around the cast iron lamp-posts was fun and spinning around in dizziness, oblivious to the dangers of banging your skull against the nearby wall. Political correctness and health and safety legislation was light years in the future for us.

Listening to the radio or wireless as it was known and visits to the local library was popular as TVs were few and far between. Mam loved going the library and read about seven books a week. Mam and Dad were the first in our neighbourhood to get a TV, a black and white model with a tiny screen. Children flocked from the surrounding area and the floor area was packed around the little box – especially when *watch with mother* was on. *Bill and Ben, the flowerpot men* and *the little weed* in the middle was popular as well as *Andy Pandy.*

Later scary dramas and science fiction such as *Quatermass* had us hiding behind our fingers spread across our eyes and face. We always seemed to have a coal fire roaring up the chimney replenished by a coalman calling every week looking like one out of the *black and white minstrel show*. Again the Echo newspaper was recycled to light the fire under wood chippings. It was used again to cover the front of the fire over a shovel to draw the oxygen into lighting the firewood chips and heaped coal. The fire was always started this way and ultimately the paper burst into flames when the new fire got going. This was a test of speed to grab the burning newspaper and shove it up the chimney before it fell on the floor or burned away.

A very risky business indeed. How we all survived before the health and safety laws came in I will never know. The fireplace was a good location to be bathed by in relative warmth sitting in a metal bath-tub as toddlers. Dad would use a large fork to make toast for us in the morning on the red hot coals. Real toast made on a fire will never be surpassed. Mam and Dad always used to warm our clothing in front of the fire on frosty or damp mornings before went to school. Dad was very handy and built fitted kitchen units in our kitchen before they were ever dreamt of in the UK. We ate at a bar type table built around the wall next to the coal cupboard under the stairs. A scary dark cupboard of hidden monsters to frighten the life out of us children as toddlers. Although born three years after the war we were still sent on errands to collect the *rations* from the local shops. Rations had finished some years before but old expressions lingered on. The local shops in Orrell, Bootle where we lived had shops of character and name such as *Tufts*, *Wormwells* and the *cockle* shop, which sold a range of local fresh fish products in small containers to nibble at such as prawns, cockles, whelks etc. Using a nappy safety pin to extricate the boiled creatures from their snail like shells was particularly interesting to us youngsters.

The forerunner of superstores was local grocer *Irwins* becoming Tesco's mega business. The local co-op where Mam got her dividend (*divi*) benefits was a place of wonder to see the money shoot off in compressed air cylinders around the shop. The local fish and chip shop (*chippy*) was always busy and again the local Echo broadsheet newspaper was recycled once more as the outer wrapping of the chippy bundle. Amazingly we all managed to survive that form of wrapper before it was deemed unsuitable and unhygienic by the brave new world of bureaucrats. Jobs-worths and Inspectors gathering in the wings waiting to emerge in the brave politically correct new world.

As kids we made bicycles from scrap bikes from better off neighbours and go-karts or *trollies* as we called them from planks and pram wheels with steering handled by a rope on the axle of the front wheels. Engine power was by someone pushing you by the shoulders or rolling down hills and inclines. However brakes were unknown and accidents many. Mam used to keep the Christmas presents hidden on the top of a lofty wardrobe in our room. One year somehow brother Jimmy managed to scale the wardrobe pre-Christmas and it fell against our bed smashing the door mirror and depositing Jimmy and the presents on the floor covered with glass. Mam came running up the stairs and Jimmy blamed the wardrobe for *just falling on him.* Jimmy was always into something and was grounded in his bed one day. He skilfully made a life-form in his bed with pillows and escaped the scene to disappear to a day of fun and games no doubt.

Mam, after some hours now feeling sorry for him took to his room the evening tea as we called *dinner* in our house. She was shocked to see his still life-form in the bed and even more shocked to detect his Houdini like disappearance but relieved when he returned home safely. Jimmy and our brother Richard are red-heads - or they were then and known for their hot-headedness and capacity to get into trouble with the authorities. Of course I was no angel. I and other boys got chased down a disused railway track by the police one weekend. We were only after the wild rhubarb that grew on the trackside. The police didn't catch us of course.

We had a procession of animals over the years as pets from tadpoles, frogs, toads, newts, snakes, an owl named Ollie (who died after eating plastic), hens, rabbits, dogs and cats. Sadly for us the hens were periodically despatched by the ringing of the neck in a quick execution by Dad to provide us with fresh chicken for dinner. Favourite hens took a bit to swallow at the dinner table, but it was impolite to leave food on the plate. We lived on big chips fried in lard in the chip pan and bacon and egg as well as traditional scouse. The food dish nickname for Liverpudlians, *scouse* had its origins based in a cheap type of Irish stew so they say. Our scouse was full of potatoes, vegetables and whatever meat was available such as lamb or mutton. It always tasted better after being rested in the pan for a day or so and being heated up. Brown *Cheerio* sauce was then applied and bread used to mop it up. A favourite meal also was brawn on chips, which seemed to melt on the chips and had a meaty but spicy taste.

Years later we were to find out brawn was made out of animal brains, which probably gave it that unique mind blowing flavour. Thank goodness *B.S.E* was unheard of then in cattle. A modern day dietician would have been horrified to have seen the high fat content lard melting with the chips swimming on top when the chip pan was heating up. Artery clogging up theory was not an issue in those days and diet and excess fats, cholesterol and heart disease links unheard of. Most of us were reasonably slim and active even though the fatty diet was a factor. Later on in life heart disease was to strike four of the brothers but perhaps the cause was genetics rather than just fatty foods. Another side effect of the cooking of the chips was the fact that Mam hung some of the washing on a clothes horse or maiden as they were called, which was hoisted by pulleys up to the kitchen ceiling above the cooking rings. Consequently when shirts were worn in our late teens and we were going to disco's and on dates we had some noses sniffing from close quarters. Although Old Spice aftershave was doused on us before leaving homes, actual or would be girl-friends would periodically refrain from close contact at times depending on the chip odour level on our clothing, clean as it was.

As children up to adulthood we had a compelling habit of reading comics and later books and newspapers at the dinner table. Mam and Dad gave up trying to dissuade us from reading at the table and consequently we mastered the use of the fork but not the knife which was abandoned so we had a spare hand to hold the comic or book at the table. Our love of reading originated from the comics we bought weekly out of pocket money and annuals such as the *Dandy, Beano, Flash Gordon, Dan Dare* etc, which were provided every Christmas in our sack by our beds. We also devoured all the reading material including Lorraine's girly books and comics as well. Christmas for all of us was magical although we were not at all well off, it was special and a wonderful family get together.

By today's standards the presents were low cost and basic but much appreciated and totally satisfying. Girly stuff like dolls and girl's annuals for Lorraine and for the boys *meccano* sets to assemble, torches to play in the dark with, simple games like draughts, snakes and ladders, more annuals to read and toy cowboy and Indian outfits with pretend guns to shoot and wigwams to erect in the garden. The Christmas presents were left

45

by Father Christmas in pillow cases at the end of the bed and large woollen socks used to house a tangerine, other fruit, some nuts and sweets and chocolate as a stocking present. The Christmas tree was always real flavouring the room with a pine fragrance. Room decorations were often hand made and a roaring fire well fuelled to provide the Christmas spirit. Until we were old enough to go with him Dad used to go alone or with friends and family to the local pub called *the Cuckoo* and later *the Linacre* pub for Christmas day drinks and roll home happy and ready for a hearty Christmas roast. When we got older we would also go with him with Mam also but only occasionally as she didn't really drink.

In those days impromptu parties with friends and relatives just happened and the kids were fully involved. One of my memories is as a young boy pinching some of the bottled stout and I ended up standing on the couch singing to the party gathered, much to their amusement. Singing was to follow my life path from that day albeit with no great success but plenty of enjoyment and karaoke experience from Bejing to the Mediterranean. Some of the dinner vegetables for our meals came from Dad's allotment, which was also his retreat with a timber hut to read the paper in and a handy pub nearby called the *Cabbage inn.* Dad used to joke that a guy who frequented the cabbage was called the *caterpillar*, because he was always seen crawling (out of the pub) every Sunday afternoon. To Dad and us kids when older a roast dinner or Christmas dinner was always appreciated more after a few pints of best bitter, mild or Guinness. Draught lager then was as far out of our reach as landing on the moon. We would often go the allotment with Dad and take a picnic of lemonade bottles filled with water accompanied by egg sandwiches. Sometimes to walk alongside the canal side and to be held safely by Dad, dangling in the water to cool off in the summer heat. Very often we would wait patiently outside pubs sitting on the step with lemonade and Smiths crisps with a blue sachet of salt in. Dad would keep checking up on us, but in those days life in the main was safer on the streets and more carefree.

Dad was originally in the Merchant Navy as a stoker shovelling coal into the roaring and insatiable mouths of the ships boilers. A hell of a job literally but he enjoyed being away at sea travelling the world. A *spirit guide* was many years later to tell me via a medium during a trip to London that Dad was always at peace on board ship and *found himself when at sea*. I was to share that love of the sea and understand how he felt. Dad was built like a body builder and he was as strong as a horse most of his life. However the asbestos used in the ships boilers and pipe-work was to deliver him minute fibres of asbestos ingested into his lungs and kill him one day before his natural time. The dangers of asbestos were known by industrialists and scientists for decades since the 1920s or so but lowly workers had no idea they were at risk.

Dad was also at risk at sea many times in his life sealed in the bowels of the ship, with his ship's captain dodging submarines during the second world. He took part in the Normandy invasion in 1945 by the Allies and lucky for us came through unscathed. However the enemy within in the form of asbestos killed him at the age of 67 years. Asbestos is still killing people around the world and around 4000 people a year die in the UK as a result. Before we were born Dad would use the small bedroom as an aviary to breed budgerigars but thankfully for Mam our Dad's pigeons were housed in a garden loft. We had a mad afghan hound named max who kept escaping and chasing cyclists. Shep the dog was the favourite. He looked like a starving greyhound but ate like a horse. If I recall the RSPCA called one day much to our disgust when some passing stranger complained the pooch was starving. The expressions on his sad face were nearly human and he sang for us when asked. He would follow our tune and howl a mournful song to the heavens, snout pointing up.

We were poor mostly but money could not buy the feeling of family we had, rich with warmth and unspoken love and loyalty. We grew up in the main wearing second hand clothes and badly fitting shoes from *Paddy's Market* in Great Homer Street, Liverpool. Mam told us to say to people that the clothes came from the posh *Bon Marche* store if they asked. Mam would periodically kit us out with new clothing obtained by a *Sturla's* cheque, which was basically a credit facility based on weekly payments to a collector resulting in high interest charges.

After leaving the Merchant Navy Dad would later work as a docker in Liverpool and Bootle docks. Dad worked hard and played hard as in those days there was a pub on every street corner and the dockers endured hard times and drank much beer. Dad told us he would dress up as stage or screen characters of the time such as *old mother riley* of cinema fame and sing and dance on a pub table to the delight of his mates.

Dad would come home dusty and smelling of different cargos of the world that he had helped unload.

The strongest smell was that of animal hides he would carry on his back down the gangplank of the moored ships. He would bring us samples of sparkling iron ore and to us as children, fascinating samples of imported commodities not seen in this country. They would be part of a home collection or showed off at school. All the dockers seemed to have nicknames with Dad as *gibbo* and really funny names for some dockers. Like the man they called the *brief* or the *barrister* who was always lying on the case. (eg on the dockside - but not telling lies in court). Another one was *batman* who wouldn't go anywhere they said without robin - eg robbing).

Dad was later to suffer a serious back injury at the docks, which would hospitalise him and take him away from us for a period to a rehabilitation home. Compensation of any value was unheard of those days. From then on money was in short supply and we got by with Mam cleaning the toilets and bars of a local pub and other work at *Jacob's Cracker* factory. We never went short of food though although sometimes oddly attired in second hand or hand me down clothing and ill fitting second hand shoes from the market stall. Once I even had to wear a second hand girl's blazer with buttons on the wrong side for a boy and an embroidered school badge from that girl's school on the breast pocket.

Mam thought it was ok but eventually saw sense when other boys laughed at me and the teachers looked on in puzzlement, although I was never into transvestite ways. I recall first leaving Mams love and care and being taken for our first day at school at Orrell infant's school. We twins cried all the first day for our Mam but soon settled down. Later we attended Bootle's Orrell primary school as youngsters and enjoyed happy times coming home with ink stained fingers from the ink-pots in our desk. We had free bottles of milk at school and straws to sup with or make things out of. A favourite trick was to suck the black ink up the straw out of the inkwell without taking it in the mouth. I was to misjudge one day and suck the ink into my mouth covering my teeth. The teacher was not too impressed.

I recall we had medical examinations each year by the visiting doctor in the headmaster's office. It was carried out in front of the head's roaring coal fire (coke was the fuel burning, which was coal that didn't smoke). Part of the examination was to check the little boy's willies as contenders for circumcision. An embarrassing process and uncomfortable. Strangely one but not both of the so called identical twins had to be circumcised shortly after the examination for the good of his health or so they said. Maybe they had a quota of circumcisions to meet then. The operation was carried out when I was about eleven years old in Stanley Hospital, Liverpool just before bonfire night on the 5th of November. The surgeon must have had lots of *tips* as a by-product of his job was a joke of mine later.

I was really fed-up in hospital as I wanted to be with my friends and family around the massive bonfire the neighbourhood would build on waste ground. I wanted to set off rockets standing in empty milk bottles and throw firework bangers at others doing the same. I recall my twin brother not being allowed to visit the ward and talking through the window of the hospital ward to him and others. Sods law and the signs of health things to experience in the future I acquired an infection in my willy and my pee hole blocked over causing many problems and much pain. The remedy was medicine and a glass rod that looked like a thermometer that a nurse trained me to shove down the penis rather like a pipe cleaner.

Only when I had assured the medical staff and (they did come flocking to see me) that I could wield this instrument of medieval torture would they allow me home. It was extremely embarrassing for myself with young nurses watching me practice the torture. One time the glass *pipe cleaner* nearly disappeared from view down my willy on the start of a long journey and a mad panic ensued to extricate it with the nurses looking on anxiously. Luckily for my future baby-making career the foreign object was removed without complications.

Taking the stitches out was also another traumatic experience and one not to savour. The pipe cleaning process was continued at home until I recovered although I had one bad experience when I couldn't pee and was in agony until immersed in a bath of hot water as per previous medical advice re my discharge advice from the ward. In desperate pain and discomfort I had to pee whilst immersed in the bath, which my Mam sanctioned for that emergency.

Our neighbourhood was friendly and everyone knew each other. The *rag man* would call every week with his horse and cart and people's old clothes would be exchanged for, shillings and pence or three-penny bits. Recycling at its best we thought. The ice cream man would turn up on his three-wheel bicycle and ring his brass bell to get all the kids clamouring for him. That part of my childhood was uncomplicated with long summers, cold winters and contentment forged by a good family with caring values setting the scene for future years to come.

3
CRAZY YEARS

I was never a pheasant plucker as the saying goes but did as a teenager work part time as a turkey plucker. Until I was 27 I lived with my family in council houses in Bootle, near Liverpool UK not far from the docks. I failed my 11 plus exam at school, which meant I couldn't go on to a grammar school or higher school with all the brainy kids. However I went on to a secondary school and had a great time amongst other things playing football with a future Liverpool FC player/manager. I left school at 15 with no qualifications to speak of except a school leaving certificate. Unknown to us my mother wrote off for job interviews for my twin brother and I. This resulted in both of us getting jobs as apprentice engineers in a large engineering factory. We often had to work shifts through the night which was hard going but sometimes sneaked off to the toilets in the early hours of the morning for a snooze whenever possible. Part of my apprentice training was in a turbocharger testing unit which meant me climbing on top of large turbochargers which were used to boost diesel engine performance on large cargo ships etc. Sometimes under test at great speeds they exploded and went on fire. We normally tested them from the safety of a reinforced bunker, which looked like a *Starship Enterprise* bridge type facility full of dials and meters. Health and safety didn't seem to be a problem in those days but luckily I survived the dangers. Luckily for me and others I wasn't blown up when in the test area checking connections etc.

As an apprentice aged around 18 our employer organised an educational week-long tour around Europe. For whatever reason they booked us to visit Bols distillery and also the Heineken beers brewery in Holland. Talk about a drinks party in a brewery. There was free testing sessions of the spirits and lager available and we promptly got drunk at both venues. Wild times followed. Walking around Amsterdam we got chatting to some gorgeous Dutch girls and on saying we were from Liverpool one fair maiden asked was I Paul McCartney from the Beatles. Not wishing to disappoint her I said I was and she went away smiling with my autograph. Well not mine as I had written it using the great man's name. Not very principled of me I admit but we all do daft things in life, especially when so young. Perhaps one day she tried to sell the autograph on ebay only to find out it wasn't the famous Beatles singer.

Our so called educational trip travelled on to Italy through the beautiful Italian lakes region of lake Como and Lake Garda. A fantastic region of which I hope to return to. Hopefully one day to return there with my gorgeous wife Karen. We stayed in Milan and visited the Fiat car factory, which was probably the only educational aspect of our tour. One of our party on the tour ended up with alcoholic poisoning due to binge drinking and had to be admitted to Milan's hospital to have his stomach pumped out. Luckily he survived to return home.

At weekends, Friday evenings and school holidays we worked for a local farmer who had a lorry loaded with fruit and vegetables, eggs etc delivering to new housing estates, which had no local shops. Effectively a mobile shop.He was very entrepreneurial and we served passing trade from the covered lorry and delivered orders to customers homes. In the winter it was freezing with the serving area lit and warmed by one small paraffin lamp. Handling freezing fresh vegetables straight from the fields was often miserable work. Dipping into potato sacks often found a few rotten mushy potatoes, which left the hands soiled and cold. I carried on working for the farmer until I completed my engineering apprenticeship aged 21.

Plucking turkeys was not very nice at all as they had recently been killed by the farm workers. We saw the executions. Often the turkeys were still warm and had various insects living in the feathers when we were plucking them ready for the Christmas dinner menu. When the farmer had no work for me he would tell me to weed the miden, which was the name for an enclosed area filled with steaming farm animal droppings and manure. Crap job to say the least with flies aplenty. Another job he gave us was to work on our hands and knees trying to straighten upright the wheat or barley in the fields, which had been flattened by the tractor wheels whilst spraying the crops.

Backbreaking work as was picking potatoes from the fields before mechanisation was introduced there in later years. Some jobs but they did provide money to spend on wine, women and song. The part time work supplemented the very low wages paid to apprentices in those days. My brothers and I willingly gave a share of our wages to Mam and Dad and made sure that every Saturday night they had a big bag of fruit and vegetables, fresh eggs and of course a big turkey at Christmas.

Very often I was out with friends enjoying the Liverpool club scene on a Friday night and after the clubs we would sometimes go to a party, the local casino to play roulette, or to a Chinese or Indian restaurant in the early hours. Consequently I often arrived with a hangover and very little sleep at my Saturday job with the farmer. My first driving lessons were on the farm driving the farmers tractor or driving the mobile shop lorry around the housing estates, hangover or not. My brothers and I bought and shared a car in our late teens and I got my driving licence when I was 17. In those days there was no breathalyser test by the police to deter drink driving. Over the years I owned a few two-seater fashionable sports cars like the MGB GT model and this seemed to attract the young ladies. I also had a *souped up* twin carb Wolseley saloon car. I do admit to taking my Dad for a drive and doing 110 miles per hour at one point in the journey. He loved the trip and we all came out unscathed.

My large circle of friends and I travelled far and wide going to discos, parties and dances around Liverpool in the 1960s and beyond. Most clubs and discos had live pop, rock and tamla motown groups and the atmosphere was fantastic. *Beatlemania* was underway and the Liverpool pop scene called the *Merseybeat* was so brilliant. Dancing to live music in my opinion beats what is on offer today with digital sourced music for young people nowadays played by DJs with earphones. In those days I often used to go on stage and sing a few songs mostly of tamla motown origin and often songs by the Drifters group or Beatles. I carried on years later with the karaoke era and sang in places around the world from UK to Ireland to China and the Mediterranean onboard cruise ships. A hobby I pursued until I decided my voice and stage nerves had had seen enough. The clubs in Liverpool were fantastic and many then had a membership system and only members and guests would be admitted. Getting membership to some clubs was sometimes difficult such was the demand. The club names in Liverpool were varied ranging from the famous Cavern Club in Matthew Street where the Beatles and other famous bands appeared. Club names included the Mardi Gras, the Downbeat Lounge, the Beachcomber, Uglys, the Iron Door, the Oddspot, the Peppermint Lounge and the so called *grab a granny* nights at the Locarno ballroom. Talking about crazy years I certainly met some interesting characters to say the least. On one girl I went out with I noticed a strange scar on her thigh and I asked her what it was. She told me it was a bullet wound from an ex-boyfriend of hers when his gun accidently went off. I certainly didn't mess her about knowing the company she was into.

Another of my steady girlfriends once approached me when I was somewhat drunk one night and asked me *would you marry me if I was pregnant ?* I said yes of course I would but I didn't take her too seriously. The next day she phoned me and said she had been into Liverpool and had paid in cash for an antique engagement ring for her to wear from the George Henry Lee department store. She asked me to go down to collect it and told all my friends we were engaged to be married. Shock and horror overcame me as I was engaged but didn't know about it. I was horrified that without my knowledge or freewill she had decided we were engaged.

Thinking that she was pregnant I did what she told me and collected the paid for ring. I was in a state of shock and in my opinion far too young to be married. My family and friends thought I was crazy but I had to play her game effectively. Later on it transpired that she was not pregnant and we parted company. She in my opinion got married on the bounce as they say and had a couple of children. Years later she got in touch with me whilst getting divorced, but things didn't work out especially when she slapped me across the face for allegedly *embarrassing her in front of her neighbours* after I had taken her a bag of food and goodies for her and the children. I hope she eventually found peace and what she is looking for in her life. Another girl I met later in life certainly embarrassed me when with her friend as a cabaret singing act beckoned me on stage to join them singing *it's raining men.* She had me unrehearsed trying to follow her dance and singing routine on stage in front of hundreds of people. I felt a right idiot. She was a great girl though and was bravely recovering from a medical condition called *Bells palsy,* which amongst other things had caused the side of her face to droop. She went off to pursue her career in Germany and other places and we eventually parted company.

One crazy night my friends and I got dressed up in fancy dress to attend a Friday night party at the Beachcomber club in Liverpool. In my wisdom I dressed as a woman with suspenders and black stockings just for a laugh. In my youthful wisdom I decided to have a lot of alcohol to boost my confidence and ended up getting quite drunk. I foolishly decided to dance on a table in the club and ended up doing a strip tease act to the gathered crowd. The next morning when I woke up I was mortified when I had remembered what I had done. I was so embarrassed but luckily in those days mobile phone cameras did not exist and neither did Facebook so my shame and embarrassment was minimised.

Out of town clubs and discos like the Kingsway, Sharrocks Hill Country Club and Toad Hall were also very popular and we were out four or five nights a week dancing and having great times across Merseyside and beyond. Years later in my thirties still unmarried and living wildly I was to meet my wife Karen at Toad Hall. I probably had too much to drink but I could see that she looked beautiful and I told her that I was too old for her when I started to chat her up. She always looked much younger than her years and still does some 30 years later. Love at first sight it was.

My friends and I partied through the Beatles and Rolling Stones years and I was an avid follower of the fashion as it was then. With long hair and sometimes a trendy beard the flower power era was underway also with hippy styles and garish clothing. At one time my twin brother and friends went to Burtons the tailors to be measured for Beatles style suits, which had no lapels and were finished with bright red lining in the jackets. Crazy now it seems but that was the fashion. We even cut into the seams of denim jeans to insert fabric to make the jeans into flared bottoms as was the style then. At one time the male fashion was wear tied scarves around the neck, which on looking back seems crazy. Some girls christened me *Billy chiffon* during that period.

I was in reality a serial womaniser, allegedly considered as tall, dark and handsome then and made the most of those years in every possible way. When people ask me I say I went out with about 250 or more women, which sounds a lot but to me it only works out to about 20 girlfriends a year on average. Compared to a charismatic friend who is a high profile net-worker in the north west who it is alleged has had 1000 or more women then my track record pales into insignificance. The detailed stories I could tell about my relationships would fill another book perhaps and would probably embarrass many, including my own family so I will not go into too much detail. However I cannot change what I was and what I am. Occasionally though, even decades later I sometimes bump into ex-girlfriends in places like local supermarkets and that is a strange experience. One in particular ignored me completely.

Over those years I always said I was looking for the perfect woman and I did of course eventually find her in my wife, the love of my life. Only problem being we are both Virgos by star sign and that means allegedly that we are labelled as perfectionists. I'm sure she realises by now that I am not perfect by any means though. However when she married me she also got my identical twin brother as her brother in law. She does say he looks different though so we are safe in the knowledge that on a dark night he cannot pretend to be me and grab a kiss.

With my close and lifelong friends, Brian and Jeff, with my twin brother Tom we often had holidays abroad mostly in Spain and Majorca in particular. It was amazing then as drinks and food was so cheap and gorgeous young women aplenty. Sometimes there would be ten of us on holiday with friends from the club scene all staying in the same hotel. Needless to say we had a ball and drinks parties in the swimming pool went down well although the Spanish police came out one evening to calm our singing down. We had a portable tape recorder on the beach playing up to date pop music, which was unheard of then in the 1960's. Young women used to flock around us like songbirds to enjoy the music. *In the summertime* by Mungo Jerry was a very apt and popular song we played on the beach and lots of young holidaymakers came to hear our beach disco.

We met girls from Germany, Austria etc and free love flowed for many as they say. We also met girls from Liverpool and our region over there on holiday. One of the guys in the party had a very close encounter with a Lancashire lady with a broad accent, whom was christened *woolly back* as likened to the sheep species. She told an unnamed guy with us: *ee by gum its like a bloody barge-pole,* which to our minds was an extremely funny comment but does need some thinking about.

At the age of 21 my twin brother Tom and I had spent a lot of our time painting and decorating our cellar at home to get it as near as possible to Liverpool's famous Cavern club. Much smaller in size of course but we had a bar at the bottom of the staircase with two rooms for our guests to dance to the records disco and generally have a great time. It was a night to remember. I met a lovely lady named Sandra, who at the time was working as a petrol pump attendant and we went out for a while. She was a very nice person and to my surprise later on presented me with a daughter named Stephanie. After her moving out of the area we lost touch and I am sorry to say that I was not part of my daughter's life. I did eventually meet her and my two beautiful grandchildren Yasmin and Tristan but things did not work out and I do not see any of them. I think about them all very much and have always loved them and always will but that is how things are. I sometimes bumped into her mum and her husband who bring us up to date with the news but I wish things could have worked out better as life is too short.

To Sandra and her husband I owe a great deal for them being great parents and grandparents and will always appreciate that. We all have regrets and sometimes take the wrong paths in life, do foolish things and I am not immune from that. Whatever happens my children are part of me and I am part of them and this bond of love will last as long as the stars shine bright in the dark sky above. That belief and bond is valid and pledged eternally also to my wife Karen, to Stephanie, Lucy, Paul, Louise, Laura, grandchildren and our extended families and friends.

On completing my engineering apprenticeship I had various jobs in line management and business improvement roles/work and method study etc in factories like Beaufort Air/Sea rescue, Berwick Toys, Meccano, Barker and Dobson sweets who made the famous *Everton Mints.* These roles provided the experience to later develop my career as a business consultant to most business and not for profit sectors in the UK. In Beauforts I was given a large 12 seat inflatable life raft which I kept at home in our cellar for some years but never did find a use for it. In Berwick Toys I was a work study/business development analyst, later Production Manager in a factory with day and evening shifts employing around 250 people. They were mostly women and I eventually had a long term relationship with a young lady I met there who was there for work experience in the office.

She was my first steady girlfriend but it ended years later when I discovered her in bed with a mutual friend one night. I went a bit wild in his house when I confronted them in the early hours of the morning and probably knocked a few table lamps over etc. The next day I went around to apologise to him in full knowledge that I had never been 100% faithful to my girlfriend, especially when she was away for long periods at University on the other side of the country.

The toy factory was booming when I worked there and sold tens of thousands of kids nurse, cowboy and so called super-hero outfits like Spiderman etc. It also sold Father Christmas suits, fabric playhouses and boxed games. One night managing the evening shift I bumped into a supervisor in a storeroom and we ended up kissing. That night I took her to the Managing Director's office for a cosy chat. As the boss was not my favourite person I thought it would be good to make full use of the boardroom facility whilst he was at home watching Coronation Street. It was Christmas and I thought what the hell life is for living. I left the job there eventually and set up my own business just down the road from the factory and started to provide services to the toy factory.

Via the Production Director who was a nice guy they sub-contracted garment manufacturing work to me and I took on sewing machinists etc. I gained skills at using and repairing most types of sewing machines and pattern making/fabric cutting in large batches for my staff to complete finished garments. I worked 7 days a week for a few years and picked up sub-contracted work making denim jeans, ladies blouses and children's wear. I also got an additional income providing work study/business consultancy services to local manufacturers around Liverpool.

Larger factories making up and selling clothing would sub-contract some of their work to us and this was called CMT work. This stood for Cut, Make and Trim whereby all the fabric, cotton reels, zips, labels and patterns etc were provided by the contractor. If say we were provided with 1000 metres of cloth and contracted to make 1000 garments and had fabric left over then it was accepted in the industry that you kept that fabric. This was in the trade called *cabbage* for some reason and out of that surplus our own label garments as a bonus could be made and sold. I often went to Manchester and other places to select and buy fabrics for making our own garments.

I viewed some fabric in a warehouse and liked the look of it and bought hundreds of metres of it. However when I got it back to the factory the sewing machinists started laughing and informed me that the fabric was candy striped nurses uniform material as worn in the local hospital. I couldn't return the fabric so I cut it up into hundreds of ladies garments and much to the surprise of my staff and I we sold all the garments –

mostly to mid Wales where the locals I presume were nursed by nursing staff in non-striped outfits.

I was asked whether we could we make ladies fashion blouses for a large manufacturer and said we could. Problem being we had never made that type of garment before. As a true entrepreneur I looked for a solution and went to visit a fashion store and bought some ladies blouses. I took them back to the factory and unpicked them and made patterns, which I used to cut out some new garments using fabrics I had bought. My machinists made up the samples and I took the finished garments to the manufacturer and was promptly given some large orders. Never say no or cant do is the key in any business.

Whilst running the factory with a day and evening shift I was also driving around the north west of England and Wales with a large van as a market trader selling my garments. I also had a second market stall were I sold wicker ware and rugs, which were very popular at the time. My sister Jean and occasionally one of my girl-friends mothers helped me. It was hard work with me leaving home around 5.00am in the morning and setting up the metal framework for the stall and unloading the van/setting up the sales displays in all weathers. From Great Homer Street market in Liverpool to near Butlins camp in north Wales, to Bangor, to mid Wales we travelled. Often we slept in bed and breakfast accommodation but I do recall my sister and I sleeping in the van on goatskin rugs that we were selling. Comfortable but a bit smelly as it turned out. Smelt like a billy-goat the next morning.

Running a business and employing people was certainly enlightening in respect of experiencing people's strengths and weaknesses. One sewing machinist I employed was having problems at home and I moved a sewing machine to her home to enable her to earn additional money. She repaid me some time later in kind when I caught her stealing garments from my factory during a spot check. Stock was going missing and she was the thief. Another machinist took me to an employment law tribunal after I spoke to her politely about her always coming into work late. She walked out of the factory in a rage and told me to *stick the job* into a sensitive place on my body. The hassle of going to a tribunal was so time-consuming and annoying. Her claim was eventually rejected as *frivolous and vexatious.*

As part of my crazy years again I was running my own business a bit of a lad as they say. The day shift supervisor used to come in early in the morning when I opened up and promptly seduced me before the staff got in − or something like that. Better than a full English breakfast to start the day some may say. The evening shift supervisor was of a similar persuasion and invited me to her home one night. She disappeared upstairs that evening and came down dressed in suspenders and revealing underwear with a video under her arm.

The video she told me was passed to her by her policewoman friend who had had confiscated it alongside other pornographic goods from a dealer arrested by the police. She put the video on and I pondered whether this was the only way to get productivity up in my factory. On that I reserved my judgement and carried on fully supporting my team to the hilt. Another lady in the factory became pregnant, not by me I might add and she had the face of an angelic nun. We used to go for runs in the car into the country and I would respond to her kisses right up to the last stages of her pregnancy. We never did make love but it was surreal her wanting to be with me when another mans baby was inside her.

I met some fascinating women and experienced many situations that people would find unbelievable even with one girlfriends mum flitting with me when we were alone. On another occasion I was in bed with a girl who was based at a teachers training college in North Wales, when her friend in the adjacent room put on the William Tell overture record. The fast pace of that classic as a sensual backdrop does need some thinking about. Some may call me a love rat or something similar but I followed my genes and it seems my libido as a single man by working hard and playing hard.

Talking about genes my mam and dad were fantastic and helped me out in financial and practical ways in my business venture. Dad as a retired docker and boiler room man at the local Walton prison was of great support. When I worked at the toy factory I took some components over to the jail to be assembled by prisoners and met my dad in the jail, which was quite interesting. Luckily of course he was not an inmate and came home every day then. Back at home we have a large clock over our brick mantelpiece in our cottage type kitchen. Dad brought that clock home from the jail and said it was from the jail canteen. He said that probably thousands of inmates had been watching time, doing time over decades. Over the same fireplace at home we have a fireplace brass rail from my mothers childhood home near Scotland Road in Liverpool. Both family mementoes I often touch and I send my love to them both in my thoughts

Dad used to come to the factory to help us lay the fabrics up on the cutting table and generally help out. One night at home he woke up vomiting blood and was taken to hospital with a bleeding stomach ulcer suspected. Prior to that he had no real symptoms that he complained to us about apart from he saying to me when we were out having a pint that he had a slight pain in his chest. He was a little bit sick that night as I took him to visit his mates at various local pubs by the docks. He was in hospital for a few days and on returning from a 100 mile trip to a factory my car engine seized up on a motorway.

As a result I couldn't visit dad in hospital that night and got a call the next day to say get to the hospital quickly. He died before I could get there and all I could do was kiss him goodbye and give him my love. The so-called ulcer was actually lung cancer caused by his contact with asbestosis all his working life. Life was not the same from that point on but I got on with my life as he had wanted me to. I and my staff in the factory missed him and the business was not the same without his presence and encouragement.

I had trusted people probably too much and an economic recession was looming with people going out of business and owing me money. I foolishly trusted two market traders who took a lot of my stock on credit terms. They had always paid me on time previously but after building up my trust they as they say did a runner. They went off to Germany and I never got my monies back from them. Times were hard and I developed cash flow problems waiting for people to pay me. My overriding priority was paying my employees their wages. One day the taxman turned up unannounced at the factory and told me he had a bailiff waiting outside to take some of my possessions in lieu of tax bills. I made him a cup of tea and got talking to him. I discovered that because of his short and portly frame he had problems buying trousers, which fitted him. I swiftly suggested that I make him some trousers in our factory.

He eventually sent the bailiff away and brought back a pair of his trousers for us to make patterns from and we kitted him out with trousers that were made to measure and fitted him well. The tax bill demand was withdrawn to a much later date giving me time to settle it and both parties were happy, with of course the exception of the bailiff who was left twiddling his thumbs.

I eventually had enough of working 7 days a week with people owing me money and wound up the business eventually paying all my debts off. However not before another tax collector called at my home months later to obtain payments. At the time I had just got out of the shower and the sight of me near naked probably hastened his speedy departure from my doorstep. I suppose that encounter set the scene. Many years after various health challenges affecting our bank balance still yet another tax collector called at my home.

As it happened I had just got out of hospital after a life threatening internal bleeding event, which was extremely rare resulting in emergency major abdominal surgery and a traumatic, gruelling 10 day stay in hospital. My wife asked the tax collector in and I politely explained my situation. I was in my dressing gown and to prove the point I gave him sight of my fresh and colourful surgical incision and battered wound area. On which he turned a whiter shade of pale and green and beat a hasty retreat. The Inland Revenue wrote to me and kindly wrote off the outstanding tax bill, which shows that if you bare all and are open with them then they will be reasonable and act with compassion when needed. Many of my other experiences during those crazy years cannot be repeated here but we are all human and have our strengths, weaknesses and impulse moments.

4

LITTLE WOODS TO CHINA

I quickly moved from self-employment to working for the Littlewoods Plc, chain store division, based in Liverpool but travelling the UK. Littlewoods then had around 110 large, mostly high street stores including Marble Arch and Oxford Street stores. At the time I worked there the sales turnover for the stores division was around £650 million. The Moores family owned the chain stores, Littlewoods football pools, and a thriving catalogue mail order company. It was a great company to work for. I was taken on within the group productivity services department specifically to work with suppliers, stores, head office staff and warehousing and distribution to effect cost savings and improve profitability. The team I worked with were really good friends and we had a great time. My boss was entertaining, a gambler, drank to excess but was brilliant at his job. His boss was of a similar laid back profile and had a relaxed approach to the management of the team. In fact they used to disappear to the pub for two hour lunches and return to the office in a merry state. The boss often encouraged me and others at lunchtime to spend a few hours with him at the local casino during afternoon working hours. It was difficult to refuse as he was very persistent and he was also into not turning into work when we were working on site away from home at different locations around the country. Other members of the team were covering for his hangovers and failure to turn into work and one night I tried to point out the error of his ways. I tried to encourage him to carry out his managerial duties but he threw a punch at me and I gave up trying to steer him on the right professional track. His boss didn't really care so I had to fall into line as the rest of the team did.

One afternoon whilst working in London the boss gave us the afternoon off and we went to see the show *Evita* in Londons's West End. We were staying in a 4 star hotel for nearly a year Monday to Friday with an indoor swimming pool and very often we would put a table and chairs in the pool and sit there drinking gin and tonics. The company was paying for our lifestyle and we partied most nights with my expenses paid to me being more than I was earning in salary. I wore the best that was fashionable then and met some great people from around the world who were visiting London. One evening after work we were drinking in the bar and we got chatting to two ladies from the Lebanon. One of them told me I looked like her husband and asked me back to her room to show me a photograph of him. Taken by surprise but always willing to build up Middle East links I went back to her room. Her husbands photo was produced and he to me appeared fat and ugly. So much for her comparison I thought but she turned out to be very sociable that night. I also met a lovely air hostess, a TV executive and young lady from Norway, who was recovering from cancer and we became good friends. One night a party of women arrived in the hotel from northern England and as we had a lot of Scandinavian tourists in the hotel I decided to play a game on the ladies. I asked a couple of my work friends to go along with me and pretend to be Norwegian. In the months spent staying in the hotel I had picked up a couple of Norwegian phrases.

With a strong Nordic accent and a stilted use of English I attempted to chat up one of the visiting English girls staying at the hotel. In broken English I said I was from Trondheim, Norway and that we were drilling for oil around the London area. I explained that we had flown in by helicopter and landed in Hyde Park. She sadly took it all in as factual as her friends did. Eventually after about an hour of deception I explained that we were from Liverpool. We thought they would laugh as being taken in by some *Scousers* but the girls were quite annoyed and didn't see the funny side of it. Needless to say we never did it again. Actually we had to be quite careful what we said and did in those days as our play hard boss had a strong Irish accent and tensions were high because of an ongoing terror campaign, with bomb threats etc by the IRA in London and elsewhere. We were actually told by the staff in our hotel that police had even visited the hotel in respect of investigations around the London terror campaign.

As well as mischief making and spending our employers monies paid to us in salaries and expenses we did however manage to save the company substantial amounts of money, increase productivity/profits and reduce costs. Before

Littlewoods chain stores had sophisticated profit analysis computer software systems I was commissioned to investigate the food sales department contribution to the business. Within the mostly clothing and household goods most stores had a food hall in prime store footage selling tinned goods, groceries, cheese etc. The study took me about 6 months to complete and I discovered that the £110 million or so sales turnover from the food halls was running a loss to the company in excess of £15 million per annum.

I analysed all the related costs for running the food division including store footage costs, staffing, head office cost allocation, distribution, food wastage etc. I arranged a presentation of the findings to the board of directors and presented the bad news. The response was surprising, they were sceptical and didn't believe me, although my team and I had validated the results. I think they just didn't want to admit their ignorance of such a vital aspect of the business. One director actually said to me that the margin on the food was around 10% and that should make a profit of £11 million. When I presented my analysis of costs taking everything into account I showed that £26 million of company costs were directly attributable against the food division. I politely pointed out that although there was a theoretical margin the reality was that the net profit was actually a net loss.

One director asked me why we needed to know what the net profit was. I was amazed at his question and left the meeting bemused. In my consultancy career I found myself in similar situations presenting the facts to business people, charity managers and politicians and that advice being disregarded. Many of them just wanted to hear what they wanted and failed to open their minds to the reality and practical options available to assist them.

In Littlewoods I was getting bored with my job trying to save the company and went to see a senior director about career opportunities. He promoted me to work building up systems on a new multi-million shopping development called *Inside Story*. One the board of directors asked me to sit on their monthly board meetings ostensibly to produce the board minutes. Problem being the other board members considered me as a fully participative board member and kept asking me questions and seeking my opinions on most subjects. I was extremely nervous but mindful of the great experience it gave me.

In fact one of the directors after a meeting actually said to me *Bill, you look so cool and calm at these meetings*. This surprised me and I said Trevor, *Iam a nervous wreck inside* as I was very often. He was surprised at my comment. However we all put on a brave face on in our lives from time to time. The unprofitable food division was eventually removed from the stores and eventually the whole chain store closed down some years after I left the company. I took voluntary redundancy on the Friday and had my first self-employed job on the following Monday.

My work was varied and interesting working with start-up businesses up to Plc level clients/household names including interviewing executive directors at ASDA stores Plc head office for business development and working with most business sectors across the UK economy. I worked with green technology entrepreneurs, recyclers, private and public healthcare/NHS from A&E Dept, maternity to reviewing mortuary services at one hospital. In one pathology department a lab technician told me he could actually detect cancer by smelling bodily samples provided by patients for analysis. I spent some time in the NHS carrying out consultancy work wandering through storerooms full of jars of preserved human foetuses, peoples brains and other gory bits undergoing research. I did some work at an explosives factory, which was scary. I also did a lot of free support work on my own and with others in organisational development and grant finding for charities, social enterprises, hospices and individuals. On top of that was my unpaid political consultancy, which left me out of pocket but gave me a rare insight into the world of Downing Street and Westminster species.

One of the highlights of my life experiences was an invitation to join a party of businessmen and politicians on a 10 day visit to China. It was ostensibly a trade mission and organised by a rich Chinese businessman named Lee who had homes in both China and near Manchester, UK. It was an all male party of around 10 guys including one who I believe made and sold coffins for a living. He had me sized up from day one. For me it was quite scary knowing my heart condition history, the length of the flight and the possibility of my falling ill in a remote part of China. But I thought life was for living and I had always taken risks.

In the party were some really interesting guys and we soon became friends. One nice guy was TV show host and journalist Tony Wilson who was a well known presenter on regional TV and radio who had founded a famous Manchester night club called the *Hacienda*, co-founded *Factory Records* and had two films made based on his life. Sadly Tony was to loose a fight against cancer and die at the age of 57 some years after we returned from China. I still have a photo of us on the great wall of China sharing a joke with Tony. Shortly before he died I phoned him and he told me he was driving through the Nevada desert in the USA. He had a strong spirit and a good heart and can never be replicated.

On our trip we went to Hong Kong and a city to the east of the country called Nanning. In Hong Kong I bought my family some designer goods, or at least that's how they were branded. In one market place they invited me up a lift into a warehouse to look at designer handbags. Whilst up there alone on the seventh floor of the building with one Chinese guy I thought as none of my friends knew where I was I could have been mugged or worse. I got out unscathed but it did make me think at the time. Whilst in Hong Kong the organiser of the trip invited me to have lunch with him and his daughter on his yacht at the yacht club in Hong Kong harbour. It was a great experience and whilst there I thought wow, From Liverpool dockland to luxury yacht. My mam and dad would be pleased with my life's progress I also thought.

I vaguely recall doing some singing in a karaoke bar and later on the trip when we flew to Nanning we visited a university and on finding that I came from Liverpool the students asked me to sing a song. I sang, probably quite badly *Unchained Melody* from what I remember. I was of course ahead of the game in respect of my email friend – Cherie Blair who some years later in 2003 was reported in the media as singing to students also at a university when she was in China with Prime Minister Blair. She did sing a Beatles song however.

In Nanning our party was treated like royalty. The local politicians who we were told controlled the city and region of a greater population then the UK – in excess of 60 million people made us very welcome. Crowds waving banners and flags with soldiers and police at the roadside welcomed us. It was amazing. We had dinner with the politicians and were invited at the end of the dinner to dance with the mostly male politicians, which was quite surreal and I still have the photographs to prove it. The interest from the Chinese in England and to practise the English language was amazing. I did suggest to Lee the organiser that perhaps interest could be developed by British companies in investing in the build of effectively an English shopping mall or village with English pub, language school and English brand retailers. The idea was for all within that zone to speak English and encourage/develop language skills as well as trading opportunities. I thought it was a good idea but 10 years or more on it has still to happen.

The Chinese people were friendly and lovely with many beautiful Chinese women attending the events. I was told by one beautiful lady that she thought I was very handsome, but I didn't tell my wife that. Our party stayed at a luxury hotel with a health spa and massage facilities etc. I was led to understand that on offer by some of the spa women was more than a body massage but I certainly did not take up that option. However I believe the final bill for the hotel included substantial charges for additional services. I did book a massage though just for the experience. I was asked to undress and an old Chinese guy took a sponge out of bucket of water and started scrubbing all my private parts down prior to the massage. It was like having a brillo pad rubbed against sensitive parts. I followed up with a shower and massage and that was as far as I wanted to take it.

I had a bit of a panic thinking about aids being reported in China and wondering could that be passed on from others who had the brillo pad treatment. That is if it touched or caused a broken skin entry point for the infection. Luckily that is not the case and I am still here to tell the tale. We did discover that allegedly the local barber provided young prostitutes and we joked that one of the guys had his hair cut 4 times that week. True or false – the jury is out on that case. We were taken out to the countryside and that was fascinating. In one market there were live rats in a bucket on sale on a butchers stall, with other strange reptiles on sale. A brilliant country to visit and I hope to go back there one day. Lets see what fate brings.

5
TWIN PSYCHIC

One Friday night in October 2005 I was feeling absolutely exhausted but was mindful that I hadn't seen my younger brother Richard for some time although he was only a twenty minute drive away. As my wife was driving to visit her Dad in Liverpool I asked her to drop me off at Richard's house by Aintree racecourse. By 8.00pm we were in his local pub with me feeling somewhat revived on a diet of brandy, draught Guinness and Richard's positive attitude to serious health problems he and his wife had faced and was facing. The pub had a karaoke night and I got up and gave a song. Bearing in mind that there was nobody in the pub who would know me and my embarrassment would go unnoticed if the song was really bad.

We had decided to abandon the car in the pub's car park and get the train home when Richard's son Alex and daughter Rachel joined us for a drink. Later we went back to Richards house and were joined by a married couple who were his neighbours. By then I had enough to drink and was very hungry. After a rushed sandwich I got talking to the man and his wife in the kitchen and perhaps unwisely gave a slightly drunken psychic reading to the wife. I identified that she had a lot of emotional pain in her and that she was torn with guilt about the death of her father. I tried to reassure her about her support and love for her Dad prior to his death. She asked me if I knew how he died and I immediately reached to my stomach and patted it. She confirmed he had cancer in that area and I went on to suggest that he had a heart condition, which she confirmed.

I told her that her Dad was ok and happy where he was, to which she replied that a clairvoyant had used exactly the same words with her some time before. I also told her correctly her middle name and named her brother David who was I thought suffering a serious illness. I told her it was his liver, which she confirmed and gave her his exact age. I also pointed out the family involvement in a market stall business, which they confirmed. Yet again I had had a few drinks but was sober enough to be as shocked as they were to get so much right on our first brief meeting. To complete the night – by then it was about two in the morning I said to the lady that she had to get rid of her guilt about her Dad as she had been a good daughter and move on her life knowing Dad was in a better place free from pain and illness. In the presence of her husband I put my hands on her shoulders and asked her to close her eyes.

I asked her to imagine a white light moving slowly from her toes travelling through her body to her head and her pain and unnecessary guilt being eased and eventually ending. She was quite amazed to tell me and her husband that she could see and feel the blinding light within and was made speechless and transfixed by it until I released my hands. Again we were all amazed and surprised at what was experienced. I hope I can follow up with her to see if she is making progress in search of peace of mind and a better life.

Telepathic type occurrences for me seems to occur on a random basis and very often it is in ordinary situations over simple things like me going to the supermarket till and often knowing to the pound the cost of the weekly shopping before the till operator asks for payment. On one occasion in 2005 when my wife and I were waiting at Tesco's main checkouts some thoughts came to me about the national lottery ticket being printed at the till. Almost instantaneously the till operator informed me that as of that day Tesco's were providing lottery tickets to be purchased with the grocery purchases. My wife was with me and shrugged it off but again how did I know after years of lottery sales that a brand new system was to be offered to me within seconds of me thinking about it ?. There was no previous advertising or posters to advertise it to the best of my knowledge.

I bought a lottery ticket with the new system at that till and won ten pounds. At home I occasionally practised telepathy with members of the family by asking them to think of colours in their mind and for me to guess those colours. I also visualised colours and asked the children to tell me those colours after I had concentrated hard to send individual colours across in my mind. For some reason it worked really well with my stepson Paul, who between us managed to get five out of five mind messages on the colours correct one day. I suppose the odds against getting all five in the correct sequence are millions to one like the lottery.

In 2003 I decided to seek further advice and made an appointment to visit *The College Of Psychic Studies* in Queensbury Place in London. Founded in 1884, the College is an educational charity set up for the purpose of investigation into, and the exploration of, psychic phenomena and related spiritual matters including healing. I was interviewed by a very distinguished lady who asked me searching questions and I subsequently became a member of the College. The College is a mine of information and runs a variety of courses for those interested as I was in psychic development.

I booked to see a *trance medium* at the College in 2005, who for one hour provided me with lots of relevant and accurate information. Some of which I will relate as following: She told me she was there to offer guidance, to answer doubts or confusion, to offer encouragement, hope and light and provide a sense of direction. I was told that we are all made of energy, which is indestructible and that for me the spirit world is as natural as the existence we are now in. She said she would take a snapshot appraisal of me described by her as me having a heavy heart walking away from a situation leaving a particular situation in the distance. This of course could apply to any one of us. She went on to say that she could see *some scars of the heart centre and around the throat of the emotional level,* which in medical terms was pretty accurate as past and future challenges would confirm. I explained that I couldn't understand how I knew the private details of some people's lives etc. She said *I was very spiritually connected, well guided and uncannily accurate and I also have a lot of healing energy around me.*

I replied that I thought I had a small gift but wasn't sure how to develop it further. She said that I was basically too modest about my abilities and suggested that *I can have a tranquillising effect on some people and should develop the healing potential and said she knew that this ability to counsel and help people had been confirmed by the people who had savoured this gift.* In the political arena she suggested that I *am more linked to give myself to the collective* eg the many rather than individuals. She said I was *very intuitive and was being guided* and advised that *I should always follow the inner urge*. She reinforced this point by saying *if the heart or inner desire says follow that urge then go for that experience. Listen to the inner voice and not the voice of logic, which is engineered by environment, convention and all sorts of other pressures.* She suggested that *I was very good at writing, very good with small children and one day I will be inspired to write for children and in particular an adventure story*. She told me *I was well connected with the sea and water,* which was true bearing in mind the potential drownings and my love of the sea, lakes and rivers.

She told me stuff about my mother and father, which was accurate and other people who had left this world. She also advised that I was getting support in this world from another place and described ways to help me develop healing abilities. She finalised the session by encouraging me to move on with a healing type role in life in no matter what form it took and that help would be there for me. She was the person who told me that we didn't go on to become spirits when we die but said that in this life we were spirits already in human form. I thought about what she said and was inclined to believe her as we often talk about our soul, soul-mates, etc and he or she lacking or having spirit. She also said something, which stuck in my mind and which I now relate to other people. She said do not forget, *life is a series of experiences and not a series of successes or failures.* Maybe some great person had made that statement before and she was restating it. I know Henry Ford the founder of the American car giant said something similar.

In 2005 I attended a one day Psychic development workshop at the College and tried to read one of the few men who were attending and he tried to read me. I couldn't get anything right with him apart from one thought which he confirmed about a long train journey which he was about to embark on the following morning. He was not too good reading me either and I must have had a negative effect on him as he disappeared at lunch time and didn't return for the afternoon session. After lunch I did a reading on two ladies and was accurate on many things including job type, alcoholic boyfriend, driving lessons started for the middle aged woman and other personal details. At another psychic development course at Regent's College in London the following day I spoke to a course delegate I stopped who was walking past me as I could see a lot of sadness in her eyes over the morning session. She thought she was good at hiding her sadness but her body was telling me another story. She told me her Mum was seriously ill and her Dad was facing many personal problems and a lot of stress and responsibility was loaded onto her.

The course was hosted by TVs *This Morning* special programme presenter and past life regression expert Andrea Foulkes, the lady decided to seek further help with Andrea. At a cost of £100 per hour per consultation I hoped she would move forward with Andrea's support. The workshop was not that productive from my point of view but Jo, my niece who is gifted with psychic ability seemed to enjoy the day. I asked Andrea about my own development and ideas I had to help people. She seemed preoccupied and not too forthcoming apart from suggesting a consultation with her in London at her hourly rate of course.

I like most men I suppose had always been reasonably suspicious about clairvoyants and mediums. However I felt a strong compulsion to visit a clairvoyant to seek some answers and perhaps guidance as to my psychic happenings. I had heard about a lady living in my town who was supposed to be a very good clairvoyant/medium and made an appointment to see her. The night before I was due to see her I had a thought in my head just as I was dropping off to sleep about the clairvoyant having a pain in her right shoulder. When we first met the next morning I said *perhaps this may sound strange but I believe I may be here to help you*. She asked me *did you bring a tape with you* and I didn't have a clue what she meant. It seems that it was the usual practice to tape record the session for the client to refer to in the future. She gave me a pen and paper and went on to read me.

She was pretty accurate looking back at my notes and mentioned *far east travel* which was true as I visited China not so long after that. She mentioned various names and events and New York which all connected accurately and the fact that I would win a particular medical battle which did happen. She mentioned a Channel 4 connection, which of course did happen, said I would do some writing, which was indeed an unfulfilled ambition, talked about world events issues, which were not specified. Perhaps my comments to Cherie Blair in later years about Iraq, Israel and Darfur were relevant to her reading of future events. She also said *I would be amazed at the bigness of it all*, which still baffles me. When she finished the reading I again mentioned about me feeling I was there to help her and she told me about an alleged botched operation, which left her with allegedly many problems and a pain radiating from her head from the operation wound site down to her right shoulder. So it seems I was right in my remote diagnosis with her for some reason. She went onto give me all the gory details and the background to other challenges she was facing. I did my best to help her but whether I achieved anything I don't know. I arranged to see her again some months later, mainly to seek advice on what to do with my own limited abilities. On this second visit I obtained a lot more detailed information about myself from the reading and she picked up my links with MPs, Parliament etc and said I would be involved with people's rights, which did happen. She also brought up TV and radio involvement, which I experienced and other personal stuff I cannot relate. She said I would make a wonderful healer and hopefully that will happen one day. She also mentioned the spirit world connecting with me and other matters of detail from my past and in the future.

One thing that really annoyed me though was that she forecast when I was going to die and told me how long I had. That was something I certainly didn't want to know and didn't want it to come true until I had achieved my life mission. I wasn't so much afraid of dying as I had faith I would move on and meet mam and dad and others. However knowing is another thing. I did resent her telling me that fact and thought it was unfeeling and professionally unethical. Stupid insensitive woman I thought. I had a good mind to report her to the spirits in the sky but never got round to it. However her prophecy on that detail has long past with me outliving the forecast. She also told me some of her client names, some of whom I knew, which again I thought was not ethical and breached confidentiality. There was an intervention of a strange kind though during the reading as the large candle burning in the room suddenly seemed to erupt like a mini Vesuvius and deposit a steady stream of molten wax onto her brand new carpet.

It was quite amazing and spooky to witness, like divine intervention or a message from the spirits – waxing lyrical perhaps ?. I was quite pleased at the mess on her new carpet I admit as I was growing to resent her for many reasons and felt she had a wonderful gift but appeared quite hard nosed and self centred. She even told me about her ignoring phone-calls from some people away anxious to talk to her who had lost loved ones. It appeared that some callers perhaps, were a bit of a *nuisance* to her, although the money she made from personal readings was well received by her. Before I left she asked me to read her, which under a normal situation could have been quite flattering, her being (allegedly) the well known and media tested professional. I related to her what came into my head and she was pretty non-committal and did nothing to encourage me or advise me on what to do with my own limited psychic skills. I left her house and waxed carpet and decided never to lighten her door again.

I once spoke to a mother still in grief who had lost her daughter to illness as a beautiful teenager a few years previous. I will call her daughter Jan although that was not her real name. Jan's Mum had many aspects to her anguish one being she was so concerned that Jan was alone in the place we call heaven and suffering loneliness there as none of Jan's relatives or family friends had actually passed away and been there for Jan when she left this world. I suggested to her Mum that perhaps for Jan in heaven time has no meaning, no ticking clock and for Jan the time elapsed until Jan's Mum and Dad eventually joined her was perhaps only a moment measured in our time. I also suggested that perhaps Jan would try to get a message to them. A few days later I was thinking about Jan and her family with my youngest daughter being a similar age as Jan.

I walked into a room and found one of three candles in a candelabra on the floor under a table, one candle was flat on the table top and one was still in the candelabra. This was strange as I had trimmed and forcibly fitted the candles myself and considered they were quite firmly in place. I spoke to Jan's Mum and started to talk about my experiences of pictures falling etc after my parents and others in the family had died. I mentioned the candles and she stopped me and said Jan's Grandmother had walked into her living room and found a candle out of a candelabra and thought it might be a sign from Jan. Jan's Mum knew what I was going to tell her and I think she as I believed it was uncanny. Being the *devil's advocate* the candles could have been weakened by the heat of the room or the sun but it was some coincidence and if the end result was some comfort for her Mum then so much the better. I thought it was a message of reassurance.

I was referred to Jan's Mum by a really special lady, named Eileen O Connor, who with courage had faced major health challenges in her life. Eileen had maintained a positive approach to life's challenges despite all and worked fearlessly for the common good. She was in my mind a shining example of what politicians should be like in public life but fail to match up to. She was a giver rather than a taker and was a tireless campaigner highlighting well researched medical dangers, especially to children and those living, working or schooling near mobile phone masts. She had a marvellous outlook on life and radiated a warm heart, an aura of goodness, a unique human energy, which I had never truly experienced before that day. She was for me an angel in human form with a worthy mission on this planet. A mission without personal gain, indeed at some impact to her physical resources, her many other commitments including her family role.

Eileen to me was one of less than a dozen people in my life who totally inspired me, hero's in my mind and unsung at that. Hero's I could relate to as benchmarks of human spirit resolute against the storms of life. Examples to us all. People like anyone else with strengths and weaknesses who however face adversity with positive thought and life mission passion. A purpose originating from within and above, albeit tempered with sacrifices made along the way. Striving and succeeding in making a positive difference in people's lives, paying a personal price no doubt but enriching the lives of many. Many touched by the ripple effect that unsung hero's create and the waves that follow.

She made me think. In this day and age it is more natural to be inward looking, focussed on the few and not the many, the nearest and dearest before other brothers and sisters of the global family. To be focussed on the consumer treadmill, paying the mortgage, living comfortably. To shrug our shoulders and think that if we don't do things then others will. Under God we have responsibilities far wider than our own horizon and that is the reality of our being, as long or as short as our life is. Responsibilities for us all, but perhaps ignored by many of us within the pace of life. Inner signposts, sometimes displayed to remind us, nagging our soul, dragging us in many directions, sometimes against our will and the will of others around us. Forces within and outside, often out of our control taking us against and around soft and harder obstacles in our path. Forces ultimately leading us through the rain to the end of our rainbow or perhaps another storm.

One night I received a call from my sister in law Pat who had lost her Mum a year or so back and was as yet unaware of my alleged psychic gift. During the call she was getting somewhat upset about her Mum and I was receiving thoughts on one name. I asked Pat who Nora or Noreen was. Pat said Nora was her Mums' chief bridesmaid/best friend from about fifty years or so before. A coincidence again but all I was aware of was the voice in my head repeating the name – perhaps as a sign for Pat to confirm what I was saying. I was assuring her that we all move on after death to another place, eventually re-unite and that our loved ones are still with us and share our pain, joys and thoughts.

Many months later in March 2008 I was recuperating on a ward following my twentieth bout of surgery or so. The day after surgery I was joking to the nurses about psychic stuff etc, which in their words *spooked them out* and I went on to successfully give the

Christian name initial of both their grandmothers. With one nurse I told her of her Gran's name who had passed on, which was Mary and she said she was known as Marie. Whilst talking to the nurses I wrote down the initial of the other nurse's Nan as 'M' also and she confirmed it was correct. With one nurse I mentioned the name Morgan and America and she confirmed she was going on holiday there with her friends – the Morgans. I also told them some other stuff about a race-course, about Niagara Falls that they confirmed.

I also explained that many years ago when working with the New Labour Party hierarchy I had prophesised to one senior party figure and a few others that Tony Blair would experience some media interest connected with a blonde lady.

I also suggested that John Prescott, the now Deputy Prime Minister would experience some significant health challenge. It was a Saturday when I was talking to the nurses and I was discharged that day as walking wounded with a seven inch incision in my left side groin. I then became the proud owner of an arrowhead scar like some tribal custom bestowing wisdom or suchlike etched into my body, albeit yet undisclosed on my passport description or compulsory ID card proposed by Tony Blair's so called advisers. The war wounds consisted of central vertical scar from belly button to groin with angled scars on the right hand and (newly etched) left side groin forming collectively an arrowhead shape pointing towards my groin. My joke to my wife and others was that if in doubt then follow the arrow and who knows where it may lead !. One amazing thing did happen in the hospital was that my surgical wound was covered by a dressing and it leaked a small spot of blood. Amazingly the blood-spot was the perfect shape of a heart and the nurses all came to see it, as they and me had never experienced such a phenomena. I believed it was a message and it gave me comfort during the days ahead dealing with my recovery from the surgery and complications that followed.

Regarding the Blair/Prescott prophecy, coincidently the following day the *Sunday Times* ran a story featuring one of Tony Blair's first girlfriend's at University – an attractive blonde. She went on to work with him in politics for a number of years and was known in the team of Labour bosses I knew as *Darth Vadar* for reasons unknown to me. The following day the Mail newspaper ran a similar story about the blonde lady he was close to in his political career. A small but significant coincidence perhaps, to be turned on its head some time later. Three days after hospital discharge I had to phone my named nurse at the hospital. The nurse was amazed at the Tony Blair articles and asked me to supply her with a copy of my psychic history. As it was later to transpire in April 2006 my so called prophesy about Blair and Prescott was to be turned on its head. Revelations appeared in the media that Prescott had allegedly had an affair with a younger blonde lady during his time in public office. He subsequently had his Ministerial Department taken away from him a month later by the Prime Minister and was subject to major ridicule in the media for his affair with the blonde lady and other alleged exploits. Of course Mr Blair was the one to have a heart problem scare and treatment and Prescott came unstuck politically and otherwise with the blonde lady. I cant remember my thoughts those years back concerning the prophecy, but perhaps my logic kicked in, overrode the *message* and I thought that no blonde lady would indeed ever be attracted to Prescott, two *Jags*, two *shags* as described by some or otherwise.

In July 2009 one of my wife's close friends came around to visit us. She is a college lecturer with an interest in current affairs and politics. In her own words she relates that meeting;

The psychic session with Bill was impromptu whilst visiting Karen. Bill was working on his book about politics. I had the opportunity to read the first draft, which I found very interesting. As I read his work Bill revealed his special gift in providing honest and accurate life information about people. We discussed the psychic and medium stuff and I said that I believed certain people could make contact with the spirit world. Bill offered to do a reading, which I accepted. We went into the dining room and it was quiet and peaceful. The atmosphere was calm and relaxed. Bill stood behind me and I sensed an energy and warmth from Bills hands. Bill spoke spontaneously about names, dates and places. This included the most important one, which was August 12th.

It didn't mean anything to me at the time but about a year later my first granddaughter Grace was born. At that time there was no indication of a pregnancy in the family and that date meant nothing. Grace was born that day August 12th which was pretty amazing. Bill mentioned a building society/mortgage, which was underway at the time with my husband and I helping our son on the property ladder. He mentioned Lampeter, which later on my father had booked to go on holiday there some months later. He also mentioned Exeter Road, which had a link regarding a family interview that took place. He mentioned Jack who was my uncle. Bill mentioned a big dog with a bloody nose. The dog in our family was actually run over in an accident and suffered a bloody nose. Bill also mentioned a black person being special to me, which was a lady named Candy whom was very special in our family in South Africa. Bill said I should get in touch with her as she needed some help. I have known Karen a long time – some 20 years but was unaware of Bill's special gift. In respect of my reading it was fascinating and extremely accurate.

She did not know where I got that information from and I certainly didn't as thoughts just come to me from a greater place than here. Time will tell on future experiences and we are all connected in this jigsaw of life, death and onwards.

6
THE PSYCHIC TWIN

Like all mankind perhaps I was destined to live a life-plan drafted before birth. A life-plan adjusted over decades by personal choices made and paths chosen. A life founded on destiny and crafted by choices to pursue good or not so good life aims, to give love or be of cold heart, to be a giver or a taker in life. For me it was a path shared as an identical twin, surviving death and battling health challenges whilst living life to the edge. Destined to save lives and experience unreal and unexplained telepathic, psychic and clairvoyant situations shared with others. A life challenge, both tortuous and blessed in equal measure. A route plan, a journey mapped into my soul before the life mission started. Some would say I was gifted with psychic abilities including periodic, intuitive health diagnosis witnessed by others.

Advised to develop the healing ability by gifted people across the country I had not met before was advice that could not be ignored. They say most people have some sixth sense and have experienced in different ways telepathy, heightened intuition or some form of psychic event. However the pace of modern life tends to suppress our soul feelings, weaken those intuitive skills, the inherent abilities wired into our pulses, which assist in our decision-making processes. Life mostly demands conformity to the norm as judged by the consumer world and scientific scrutiny seeks fact-based evidence to explain the unexplainable. A gut feeling presented in the decision-making process takes guts to put forward to others within a sound argument in debates based on facts. To admit to being psychic leaves one open to scepticism, ridicule or worse from some individuals in society, but that is a price worth paying. For myself and others fascinating psychic type events have been peppering my life and in my opinion adding flavour to my own existence with some positive outcomes for others. My elder brother tragically drowned in a canal some weeks before my twin and I were born and I was lucky enough (albeit not too heroically) to save the lives of four people from drowning. This happened over a decade in four separate incidents and is a life mystery to me as well as others.

Some ask is there a connection to one lost brother drowned, the birth of twins weeks later and the saving of lives, including the young boy in the same stretch of canal where brother George drowned ?. My prophecy, albeit affected when logic kicked in about the blonde lady and health problems relating to Prime Minister Blair and Deputy Prime Minister Prescott many years before they happened is one example of these strange, illogical and unexplained episodes. In another situation knowing the precise page numbers and precise words of advice printed in a book I had never heard of was uncanny. Uncanny to me as it was to the recipients of my thoughts replicated by words already written linking to their life journeys.

This was demonstrated in the summer of 2006 by the specific words of advice I offered moments before to a fair lady, advisor to captains of industry around the globe. My words appearing moments later already printed in her unread book. I had advised her to listen to her heart and inner voice in making a life changing decision. Before the book was retrieved from her briefcase I had told her to refer to page 78, without knowing why. An unopened book called *The Cosmic Ordering Service*. A book I had never heard of until that moment. I was as shocked as her to discover my strange insight into the unseen paragraph on that chosen page. Words written in another land, another language originally, replicating my advice word for word. Or indeed my words replicating the advice given in the book and printed some time before. An event strangely repeated later that day with another on different subject. This time with page 13 of that book having the relevance. Relevance to the dark haired man with the kind heart and formidable presence.

An event followed by other book reading insights and unexplained coincidences in the future. My progression from having some psychic ability to demonstrating mediumistic skills with validated messages passed from a stranger beyond this life surprised me. A shock also to the grieving daughter sat next to me and the others listening to my message in that room. I once met a stranger on a train whose life I knew before she told me. I got talking to her, the fellow passenger and without prior knowledge or previous discussion was extremely accurate on details about her life based on my thoughts during our contact. I was correct on her birth-date, the location of a scar hidden by her clothing, details of her pet, the pet's illness, the doll from childhood still resting on her bed at night, her boyfriends detailed profile, details of their holiday, her favourite love song, the type and colour of her car and other personal facts which came to me during my contact with her.

With another lady I identified part of her life history including her migraine attacks when younger, her planned skiing holiday, her planned trip to Madrid and other details from her past etc. In others I met over the years their past, present and sometimes forthcoming life issues would come through and I would be as surprised as they were when the details were confirmed. During the General Election in 1997 I was working for a short time as a volunteer adviser in Tatton, near Manchester with ex BBC war reporter Martin Bell OBE, future MP who was trying to unseat Conservative, Neil Hamilton MP.

I told Martin's daughter Melissa that she would marry a man who had just arrived from the Labour Party's Millbank office. She probably thought I was crazy at that time as they had not yet spoken to each other. As it turned out my prophecy was correct and in the course of time I was a guest at their wedding. They later moved to France, had children but sadly got divorced some years later. The divorce I did not see coming in my mind's eye.

On one memorable occasion I had two business ladies come to see me at home as I was giving them some free advice about trying to keep their struggling company afloat. The business concept was good in principle, but fraught with obvious difficulties not helped by one of the partners telling me she would end up a millionaire. They hadn't drawn any wages themselves for two years but a clairvoyant told the older of the two she would become a millionaire, so it must be right then she thought. As it happened their company failed a few years later after the women tried to take advantage of my generosity and loan, but that is another story. The two alleged ladies sat on my sofa and I had some immediate thoughts about them. I said to the older and more arrogant of the two, (she was definitely not my type of person) *you have a problem in the centre of your chest.* I said to the younger and fitter looking partner of the two *you have a problem with your back.*

They both looked at each other with a shocked look on their faces. The older one revealed she had a hiatus hernia and a history of problems emanating from the centre of her chest. The younger one said she had a disc problem in her spine and had problems getting out of bed in the morning because of that condition. As neither of them displayed any outward symptoms whatsoever we were all surprised at my spot diagnosis of the psychic kind. What I didn't pick up though was an underlying self-interest streak in both of them manifesting in an attempt by them to take advantage of me in particular.

Like others who have tried to take me for granted and abused attempts at generosity and good will, the arrogant and self-serving sometimes, with natural justice come unstuck. I loaned them money when their business was struggling. In the case of those two ladies they ended up with County Court orders against both of them as actioned by me probably experienced potential future problems accessing credit. After trying for a long time to make them see reason and fair play I obtained a satisfactory result. They ended up losing money in court costs and probably a bit of their soul and happiness potential along the way.

The feelings I've always had about my mortality and life mission have comfortably travelled side by side within me for most of my life. I don't know why I was pre-warned, gifted with some measure of premonition and had meticulously prepared for premature dices with death even though every aspect of my logic should have told me otherwise ?. Three months before my heart stopped I felt compelled by nagging thoughts to have the comfort of a will drawn up by a local Solicitor in the town of Kendal where I was working. Why I was made aware and made ready for my impending close shave with death and had time to prepare I will never know. My inner voice was indeed my guardian angel in some ways. After my cardiac arrest and return to the world I seemed to develop other abilities, which as a layman I can only describe as psychic.

Gifts or strange abilities manifested themselves over the years with senses or abilities it seemed, which could not be called up but just happened on a random basis. For some reason they manifested mostly with women rather than men. Perhaps my natural gravitation to the opposite sex rooted in my bachelor days of wine, women and song has some bearing on the psyche. Or perhaps women are more open minded then men and interested in the power of the spirit, soul and psychic mystery.

I have researched scientific studies on near death experience and it is suggested that those that experience a close call with death often go on to develop some form of psychic ability. Perhaps this was true in my case after I effectively died and was brought back by the angel above. However my twin brother's daughter has powerful psychic and clairvoyant abilities and she has always been in reasonable good health.

Before my close encounter with the grim reaper I can only recall a few eventful occasions other than the telepathic bond with my twin, which was my normal life. One such occasion happened after my Dad died suddenly with the whole family understandably shocked and upset. As was the practice at the time Dad was brought home the night before the funeral and was at rest in his coffin in our front lounge at home. Members of the family would go to his side and see him for the last time and say their goodbyes, alone with him and their thoughts. I was nervous, full of grief but went in to see him on my own.

I spoke to him, told him how much I, and all the family loved him and I shed more than a few tears. I cut a lock of his silver grey hair to treasure and asked him and God to give us a sign that he was ok and happy in a better place, free from pain. I asked Dad to move curtains, move a picture on the wall or do anything to contact us. Of course nothing happened and I said goodbye that night and left the room, which was previously the room of happy family parties. A meeting point for laughing children, Christmas warmth, Dad's humour, his love, which radiated to fill the home and the hearts of people in his life.

Next day after the funeral all the mourners, family and friends came back home and such were the numbers that people were scattered over the house from the front lounge where Dad was the night before, down the hall to our kitchen area. I was talking to Mam in the kitchen when we heard a small commotion from the front room. I immediately said to Mam *don't worry that is Dad sending us a message that he is ok.* Mam looked at me puzzled and we then made our way to the front room where the noise originated. It seemed that a picture, which had been hanging for years had fallen off the wall. No one was standing near the picture and I certainly hadn't told anyone about my private chat with Dad the night before. What was puzzling was that the nail was in the wall and the picture cord still intact.

At the time and indeed to this day I still believe it was a message from Dad. What is stranger even is that pictures or framed photographs standing on shelves or bookcases have periodically moved or fallen in my home soon after the death of loved ones. All these events happened within days of a death and I certainly believe that they are not coincidences when they have occurred on at least six occasions following deaths over the years. In 2009 I was with my wife visiting her cousin at her fathers home. The father had died a few days before and we were all talking in the lounge.

As tactfully as possible I was trying to reassure the family that the dad was in a place of love with his wife and that they would get a sign that he was ok. I told the five or six people in the room about pictures falling off the wall soon after the death of loved ones over the years and my belief in that phenomena. Unbelievably after about ten minutes had passed an ornamental plate in the shape of a fish fell of the wall in front of us all. For me even as a believer it was a shock, but the nail was still in the wall and the plate was behind furniture, which meant nobody could get near to disturb it.

Another strange example followed the first day of March 2006 when my Father In Law, Tom passed away after a brave battle against a previous stroke, cancer, pneumonia and the kidney disease, which he finally succumbed to. He was in hospital for some seven weeks and blessed with his four children visiting, giving love and staying with him must of his last weeks of life. The family and I said our own silent prayers for him at various times. I tried to send him healing, peace and contentment in my own quiet moments with him. Strangely though, near the end, when I looked over at Tom's face in the bed I could see, superimposed the face of my own beloved Dad who had passed on so long ago. It was uncanny but in some way a comfort. I also felt Tom's deceased brother and sisters were close to us at the bedside.

Brave and typically determined as ever Tom did prove the predictions of the renal team wrong and outlive their blunt estimate of *passing away within a day or so* and rallied around to start taking in some nourishment and to go on for another two weeks. Near the end he told his children that he loved them and they told him the same. Un-stated love was the way of his generation and upbringing, although love was felt deeply and demonstrated in many ways it was traditionally unsaid. Up till that point and spanning half a century the love word was not really spoken across the generation gap. A week or so before he passed on to a better place than his sickbed I told his grandson, Paul that I had the feeling that Wednesday and five was somehow relevant to Tom. A week or so later on the Tuesday night Tom was reasonably comfortable - as much as he could be and the Clinicians were planning his care package and treatment going forward. The next day I had an urgent call to join my wife at the hospital and broke all speed restrictions to get there but Tom had died just a half hour before. The time he died, my wife told me was five minutes past two that Wednesday afternoon. When I arrived there were five members of the family around the bed. A sad coincidence or something more perhaps.

The grief his children felt is, as for all people suffering the loss of a loved one, was a hammer blow and although feeling inadequate in making them feel better I did what I could. I said to my wife that her Dad was still around her, still aware of her great love, her anguish and pain and that he was at peace with loved ones in a better place. I said he would send a sign that he was ok. That night we returned home and I sat with my wife and his four grandchildren around a table, each of us with a glass of wine discussing memories of him. The doorbell rang and I answered the door to let my stepdaughter's boyfriend, Simon in. In the hallway was a table and a framed photograph, which had seemingly fallen face down on the table over the last half hour or so. Simon picked it up as we went to join the family and it was a photograph of Tom, my wife and her Mum on our wedding day.

I told my wife and the others that the fallen picture was a message of comfort from her Dad but whether they fully believed or not remains to be seen. Small but significant psychic happenings would drop in and out of my life without pattern or reason. Some events of importance to me and others, some trivial. One dark night at home I visualised a small mouse searching for food in our garage adjoining the kitchen. In a silly billy mood I adopted a karate type pose and opened the adjoining door, turned on the light and stepped into the garage ready for action. I don't know who was more shocked the little dormouse or me when it looked up at the foolish homo sapien ready for battle. The mouse soon disappeared though in disgust, out under the door to the garden away from my aggressive stance. Coincidence or what ? How could I know it was there? I've never seen a mouse since or before that day alive in the garage. That is apart from the dead ones that the cat brings in as offerings to the family.

Quite often the accuracy would be uncanny with this gift. Luckily for me and my credibility an ability often witnessed and validated by professional people and others of sound common sense. If I tried too hard to summon up the gift on request then it wouldn't really happen. The dilemma I had was do I keep these strange thoughts and insight into people's lives to my self or do I reveal my inner thoughts and possibly face ridicule or derision. Signs and messages of the psychic sort probably started when I was in my early twenties. I once had a girlfriend who was a very attractive and nice person but we drifted apart and lost touch. Months later she later approached me in a noisy club dance floor *The Beachcomber Club* in Liverpool to tell me somewhat calmly (or that's how I recall it) that she was pregnant. At the time I couldn't take it in because of her calmness, my alcohol intake, the informal way of contact etc.

Me being quite irresponsible at the time I stupidly put it to the back of my mind and carried on with my wild lifestyle. A big regret in my life though and something I wish I could have put right as I failed to do the right thing and take things seriously. She disappeared off the scene after that night and unknown to me she was indeed preparing as a single mum for a baby, my daughter in her life. The night before our daughter Stephanie was born I was driving with a girlfriend to local seaside town Southport and watched a beautiful sunset with golden and reddish hues. A beautiful sky in June 1970 captured as a back-drop framing the suns steady immersion into the Irish Sea. Attempting and failing miserably to be cultured and poetic I made some analogy about the beauty of the sunset, comparing the vista before us with the birth of a baby. Of course a sunrise would have been a more appropriate connection but for some reason that's what I said. I don't now why in heaven I brought a baby into the conversation but sure enough the next day I found out that my first child had been born the day previously and I was regretfully oblivious to that reality and wonderful event.

Life moved on and some years later I had a strange experience with a new girlfriend. I was living a bachelor life in Crosby, near Liverpool and she was a local girl I had recently met. She was very attractive and told me she was a model. It was the seventies and unusual for that decade she had undergone a boob enlargement operation with breast implants. She was ahead of her time in the use of cosmetic surgery and to me it was quite fascinating. I remember the thin scars well and the uneasy feel of the silicone or whatever was used then – yuk, give me the real thing anytime. One night we had gone to my local pub, the Crow's Nest and got suitably *sozzled* (eg drunk) and returned to my house for the evening. At one point the young lady disappeared upstairs to the bathroom and seemed to have been away a long time. I was sitting on the sofa and saw what I can only describe as a flash of a scene in my mind of her on the floor with blood on her. Puzzled and now getting somewhat anxious I went up the stairs and knocked on the bathroom door.

She didn't answer me so I had no alternative but to push the door in and found her slumped on the bathroom floor with oozing cuts on each wrist. She seemed a bit dazed but luckily the cuts were reasonably superficial and appeared to have been made with my blunt disposable razor. I took her downstairs and spent most of that night talking to her and trying to convince her of why she should live. She had a child and was a single mum with some problems in her life it emerged. She wouldn't let me contact any medical assistance and seemed to pull herself together and said she was ok. It was a cry for help and she assured me she would be all right and I admit to feel somewhat out of my depth in dealing with her situation at that time. It was a difficult night thankfully never to be repeated. She didn't see me again and I hoped she went on to get what she wanted from life afterwards.

I hope I didn't let her down when she needed something in her life and pray she is happy now and what she did that night is a memory locked away from the light of day. Me seeing her remotely from a point downstairs was yet another mysterious event in my life and I don't have the answer to that episode. I had an interesting experience when I was asked to take part in a slot for Channel 4 TV's *Richard and Judy show*. *Richard* and Judy presented a research item including discussion about telepathy between twins and I phoned in with some examples regarding my twin and I.

Some months later the Channel 4 production company *Cactus* contacted me and asked me whether I would like to take part in a televised film about *Psychic Detectives*. The proposal was that four or five people would be schooled for two days or so in psychic skills at the consultation rooms of a South Wales psychic named Sue. Psychic Sue had apparently built up a strong reputation as a competent psychic and worked with the police on some serious crime investigations including murders. The out of pocket costs of travel and accommodation were to be paid and as it was of great interest to me I jumped at the chance to participate. I had booked to travel from Liverpool, Lime Street, down to Swansea, South Wales and onwards to the hotel. When I got to Lime Street the train had been cancelled and I seriously considered whether it could be an omen.

As it happened I decided to carry on and went by car instead and travelled 230 miles late that night to a rather modest bed and breakfast pub booked by the film company. We met at the Psychic's office above a small shop and I was introduced to the other four fellow students and Psychic Sue. Danny Wallace was the producer and presenter in charge of the film crew from Channel 4 and he was to participate in the workshops as well as directing. Danny was an outgoing dynamic character and had recently set-up a web-site initiative called *Join Me*, which encouraged droves of people to meet in large groups in public places around the country for what seemed no particular reason apart from being part of that network. It seemed to be very successful and attracted a lot of national media attention. Danny went on to appear periodically on TV in different shows including one he presented based on his plan to start a new country with a fresh approach to political issues and governing values.

The two day psychic workshop was broken down into sessions to introduce the students to chakras, auras, tarot cards, meditation etc all of which I wasn't really comfortable with. I was there more for the practical psychic development advice, to build existing skills and I patiently went along with the flow of the workshop. I felt I had a serious reason for being there, one being that I was seeking advice about my perceived gift and secondly that I needed some pointers in how to further develop my skills – hopefully for the good of others. However I felt the filming was starting to turn into a farce.

It seemed to be developing into what I would describe as taking the piss out of a serious subject and we were caught up in the process looking like lemons. Danny as producer but also one of the psychic students was being very flippant and I felt the other students and I would be made to look like idiots for maximum impact on TV. I told them I was unhappy with the inappropriate farcical spin and nearly walked out on the filming. Perhaps we were idiots for agreeing to be psychic guinea pigs on show to millions of viewers. The camera crew had us and the psychic walking through a park with flowers in our hands. Possibly to represent some spiritual connection I couldn't quite grasp. My limp bloom was a sorry sight not to be shared with the nation I thought, Sweet William flower or not. I nearly walked off camera in embarrassment. I was dreading anyone I knew seeing the film of the park scene in the early evening *Richard and Judy show*. Luckily for my dignity and street cred the whole two days of filming only lasted for a matter of seconds on the live show. TV fame for me in the blink of an eye.

One interesting event did happen though after the psychic asked us to follow her instructions and enter into a type of trance or meditation to penetrate the mind of Dr Harold Shipman. He was the general practitioner serial murderer of an estimated two hundred or more of his own patients in the North West of England. Shipman was in jail serving life at the time of our filming and was later to commit suicide in prison, January 2004 to avoid his earthly sentence. Perhaps he went on to a different type of divine justice and a hot welcome of the retribution kind. We can only hope he fully serves an appropriate sentence elsewhere and faces some serious questions from his victims.

The gathered students, Danny and I were asked to adopt a meditative state and describe Dr Shipman's crime scenes and events that came into our minds eye. We all made contributions but to different degrees all generally aware of the media reports and details by the police and court leading up to and after Shipman's conviction. Logically what we saw or imagined in our minds was probably based on periodic media information and acquired knowledge of his evil deeds. However during the course of my journey into Shipman's mind I began to feel ill with severe nausea for some unknown reason. I had visualised Shipman's visit to a victim's house and then had to stop when he was at someone's bedside. The nausea was overpowering and I had visions of being sick in front of the camera.

Some time later I was to find a mysterious connection with the murderer. I recovered after that session and I tried a bit of telepathy with some other students, which was ok and then tried to read the story behind Danny the producer. That was pretty hopeless as I got it completely wrong he told me. That very often happened when I tried to do psychic stuff to order – it just didn't work on demand. However a year or so later I was watching Danny on TV presenting his *new country* programme and he was searching for a slogan or statement of principles for the citizens of his new Shangra La.

About twenty seconds before he made his statement the words *be good* came into my head and they were the exact words he used on the TV. Coincidence or not at least in my mind I had, I believe got through a barrier to reach his thoughts on life. Before heading home I passed over to Danny a few written thoughts about Channel 4 celebrities *Richard and Judy regarding a recent/imminent foot problem for Richard and a broken tooth or dental problem for Judy* and to this day don't know whether they occurred. The Richard and Judy show went out shortly afterwards with our psychic clip in and I was relieved it only showed a few seconds of me in the piece. The experience was a lesson about the media to remember as they clearly have different objectives than the viewing public at large. I wrote to the researcher from Channel 4 and mentioned my baffling nausea during the journey into the evils of Dr Shipman.

A year or so later I was messing about on the Internet and keyed in my own birth name. A cold shiver ran down my spine when my name appeared to leap out of the search engine summaries as a likely victim murdered by a Dr Harold Shipman. Well not me of course but a William namesake who it seems was one of the murder victims of the GP. Although murder could never be totally proven because of the cremation of the deceased the family were convinced that was the case. The web search revealed a transcript of a statement made by Mrs Rita Shawcroft, the daughter of the victim to the police and authorities. Rita lived in Hyde and Shipman was the family doctor. Rita's Dad William lived in Denton near Manchester and died at the age of 77 on 28th September 1981. In 2005 I contacted Rita by telephone, albeit rather sensitively when my name was asked. I said I was researching my family name, which in essence was the case as very few people to the best of my knowledge having that surname are resident in the United Kingdom.

Rita told me that her Dad also had a brother named Thomas also like I did with my twin brother Tom. The Lancashire connection may even be relations and that is something to follow up. Rita was understandably shocked to find out my name was identical to her dads. Rita told me she believed her Dad was murdered by Shipman. She said that her mother who was also a patient of Shipman and had died in hospital some time before of natural causes but thankfully out of the reach of Shipman at that time. For some strange reason documents relating to her mother were allegedly found in Shipman's garage however. We had a good talk and she misses her parents although time has moved on. She believes they are still around her and says good night to their souls before she goes off to sleep. I wished her well, left my contact details and hope she finds peace in this life and beyond when she is reunited with loved ones. On thinking about

Shipman he could not see anything wrong in his actions as he played God, jury and executioner for other peoples lives. It later emerged that he had probably stolen jewellery and other items from his victims. Shipman's proper title as it turned out should have been the family butcher rather than family doctor considering the great number of innocent lives he slaughtered to feed his own twisted appetite for control.

I also mentioned by letter to the researcher at Channel 4 production company – *Cactus*, that some 13 months before in July 2002 before attending the psychic detective course I had written some thoughts about the awful tragedy of the abducted and murdered schoolgirl Milly Dowler. I enclosed a copy of my thoughts in my letter and sent a copy to Psychic Sue in South Wales. I had initially written a list of around ten specific points I visualised connected to Milly's murder.

I was somewhat shocked to discover in early 2008 strong connections to my list some five and a half years after sending the letter. The Prime Suspect in Milly's case was a man sentenced to life imprisonment, early 2008 for murdering two young women in the area where Milly was living. My list of ten points including *builder, red car, Corsa car, small box van*, which I drew and *lamp*. To-date those five out of ten points on the list have been reported in the media as being directly connected to the murder suspect of Milly. The lamp connection was that the suspect was stopped by the police and he had a broken lamp on his vehicle. Back in 2002 I added another seven points to the list and mentioned *three others – victims*.

After linking and validating some of the aspects of the murder enquiry to my list my quandary was do I say nothing or contact Surrey Police and provide them with the list. I of course did not wish to be considered a crank but Channel 4 and Psychic Sue had a copy of my document in 2003 before the world had heard about the vehicles etc used in the Surrey murders. After much heart-searching and thought following renewed contact with Psychic Sue I phoned Surrey Police in March 2008 and gave them the details I had. To-date I await any follow-up.

One of the things I had written was red car – Corsa. A year or so after my letter the police announced they were looking for the owner of a car seen on CCTV camera shortly before Milly disappeared. The car the police were searching for was a small red car but specifically a red Daewoo Nexia. Coincidence probably but the small red car was a pretty close match. A Corsa car was also identified in the police enquiries. Whether the other details I wrote down will ever match up will be a mystery until the killers full profile is made public.

A classic example of the quandary I have when deciding whether to volunteer my thoughts to people I sense details about was during the first meeting I had with a senior figure from a Government Ministry when he was visiting a Southport Hotel. He was a guest speaker at a business network meeting that evening and I had asked to meet him for a chat beforehand. We had a chat over a drink and he turned out to be really nice guy, Younger than you would imagine for such a high-level Civil Service position he held but very talented, very laid back and sociable. I described him as the *Jamie Oliver* of Civil Servants – good at what he did, a warm heart and straight talking with a natural charisma. During the conversation I kept tuning in to thoughts of yellow plastic ducks of the type toddlers have in their bath tubs.

Feeling a bit daft but what the hell I thought, as he seemed a nice guy to confide in. I said *Tom, this may seem a daft question but do you have a plastic duck in your bath at home ?*. He looked at me with a incredulous look on his face nearly spitting out his drink and I then said *but you have not one but two yellow ducks in your bath*. He nearly fell off his chair and asked me how I knew such personal detail. Perhaps he thought I was having a secret affair with his wife and was familiar with his bath and secret aquatic pleasures of the undressed sort !. It seemed that the ducks were his from childhood and his own young children would use them in his bath. Some months later I was to phone him and joked that I had the feeling that one of his ducks was unwell. He told me that his wife had recently applied bleach on one of the old ducks to clean it up. A few years later in April 2005 he was to confirm by email from the Ministry in London that the psychic episode had indeed occurred as described, giving me at least a top level auditing and validation of the reading. His job title was Deputy Director, Enterprise in the government Department Of Trade and Industry. To suggest a grown man of some eminence had one duck in his bath was a long shot but to have confirmed that two ducks were regular occurrence from a childhood legacy was pretty surprising.

One evening I chatted to three ladies in a pub and ended up having a go at reading aspects of their life. The feedback seemed pretty positive that I was accurate with all three each having different life profiles and experiences to work with. I was joking with one and said I would feed some *energy* into her. I jokingly put my hands on her shoulders and a few seconds later she nearly jumped out of her skin. She said she felt something like an electric shock surge through both her shoulders via my hands. She was as shocked as I was – perhaps it was the alcohol.

On two separate occasions over a two-year period I was to be told without prompting or pre-discussion by established psychics that I would make a good healer and that was a path for me to follow as part of my destiny. That is something I intend to research. Another occasion I was chatting to Lucy my teenage daughter who was suffering a bad headache and again I was joking and put my forehead close to hers and asked her to close her eyes so I could ease the pain. I visualised a white blinding light from my head moving into her head and a red light also appeared to me during the process. I wished for the pain to come from her to me and then stopped and asked her to describe any effects she felt. Without me mentioning anything about my sensations she described a blinding white light in her head.

We were both amazed and her headache appeared to ebb away. Strange but true but I ended up with the headache shortly afterwards. In July 2004 I had to book by telephone a hotel in London for a family trip and I was chatting to the reservations lady who was some 210 miles away in a large hotel near Hyde Park in London. I had met her briefly when paying a bill once and remembered her name and distinctive accent. She was into church gospel singing, which I always wanted to experience in a live gig. I hesitantly asked about some thoughts I had picked up from her about her planned Italian holiday to Rome and she couldn't understand how I knew the details. Indeed she had booked a holiday for her mother and family the previous day to Rome.

I went on to tell her, her suitor and eventual boyfriends name – Graham, her brothers name – David and other personal information that amazed her and me in the process. I spoke to her some time later and she said her mother found it difficult to believe I knew all the details, but she believed me when I said it had just come to me. Psychic things keep happening in my life and come and go like shooting stars in the night and day sky of my being.

7
HEALING WAYS

In 2006 I responded to an advertisement in the local newspaper, the *Liverpool Echo* regarding a new psychic development evening class starting in a beautiful old building in historic Hope Street, Liverpool City. The area is in a preservation zone and the buildings and sense of tranquillity in the heart of Liverpool quite amazing. I joined the weekly class of about twenty people hosted by two experienced psychic/mediums. Agnes from Aintree, Liverpool took the lead role and she was well respected and a lovely person as it turned out. It was good to be amongst like minded people, all there for different reasons and some obviously dealing with health and other challenges in their lives. Female students were in the majority with only myself and another male attending on a regular basis. He was a really nice guy who was a plumber by trade and I joked that he could advertise on his van as *psychic plumber – we will find your leaks before they happen.*

As the weeks went by I did feel that my psychic ability was developing slowly as experienced within the evening class and in day to day life. Coincidences or otherwise seemed to become more frequent. One example was when I was having my haircut and chatting to the young hairdresser Nick about the psychic stuff, of which both he and his mum were interested in. As he was cutting my hair I was joking to him about a Government Minister I met some years ago named Tessa Jowell whose husband was front page news in all the newspapers and the media in 2006 regarding allegations about financial links to the Italian Prime Minister – Belusconni. I told Nick about the first time I met Tessa in 1997 with me saying *hello Tessa I'am tosser*.

It was a joke however about the tosser bit but I did meet her and had a good talk with her about politics and thought she was quite sexy in a funny sort of *on message* way. Whilst I was telling Nick about the meeting of Tessa and tosser. my mobile text message service rang. My mobile phone was in my coat jacket on the coat stand behind us and I paid Nick and said goodbye. I left the hairdressers and called up the text message on the mobile phone. What amazed me was that it was a joke text from a local political figure/high profile friend of mine, which said that the worlds largest pancake was being prepared in Liverpool and all that was needed was some volunteer tossers to come forward to toss the pancake on the flames. It was clearly a joke as tosser in the local vocabulary and beyond is clearly a derogatory term originating in male only habits. I walked back into the hairdressers straight away and showed it to Nick who was amazed as I was with the simultaneous Tesser/tosser dialogue.

Yet again with another hairdresser some weeks on I had the word toe nagging at me whilst she was working on my haircut. I said to her *have you got a problem with your toe*. She was amazed at my insight and said that at the end of each working day one of her toes gave her a lot of pain and discomfort. Discomfort not obvious to anyone during the day and she couldn't figure out how I knew. Her boyfriend was quite sceptical when she told him and some weeks later he spoke to me about it and I said I had some news for him regarding a visit to the doctor.

I said *lower back pain and knee* of which he confirmed as he had some days before been to see his GP about those problems. He was pretty speechless and I breathed a sigh of belief that my instincts or whatever it was were in this instance accurate. At subsequent psychic development classes I was pleased to give a pretty accurate reading to the course tutor/psychic-medium of facts around her and her family, which she told me was 95% accurate. My confidence was building. At a later session the students were asked to bring in a photograph of a deceased person for others to give a reading on.

I was passed a photograph and was asked to say what came into my thoughts. Just before that a new person to the course entered the room, registered and sat down before me. I looked at the photo and said: *Margaret, married to a Scottish man, naval career, three children, five grandchildren, loved baking pies etc, ended up disabled in a wheelchair, died of cancer, much loved and loving to her family with warm heart*. I mentioned other family names etc and finally said that I could see someone visiting her grave and still grieving. The tutor asked for the person who brought the photo in to reveal herself and to feedback whether the reading was accurate or not. A lady said the photograph was her

Nan and that she could only relate to the baking of pies comment, which I agreed was a general activity for her generation.

However the lady sitting next to me, now in tears explained she had joined that night because of the loss of her mum and that the name Margaret and everything else I said was indeed about her mum and family. The messages I got were about her mum and not the lady in the photograph. She was amazed as I was but satisfied with the thought that messages from beyond were so accurate that they must originate from her mum now in a better place and free from pain and disability. Since that night frequent occurrences that I can only describe as psychic or telepathic occur it seems on a more regular basis. However the new doorway, which has opened to mediumship is a new pathway, both scary but exciting at the same time.

Leading to who knows where ?. Feedback from the two psychic mediums I met, one in London, the other near Liverpool both independently mentioned they had picked up some healing abilities in me. That led me to attend workshops run by the UK *Healing Trust,* which gave me an insight pursuing part of my destiny. Occasionally I would use a friend's office as a hot desk facility for writing my book as I found it frankly a lonely experience and with too many distractions penning the book from home.

Hanging the washing out and hoovering to name a few distractions. One young lady, Lucy in my friend's office was complaining of a pain in her shoulder and I mentioned to her about my alleged gift of healing. She agreed to let me try some healing on her in the office meeting room. In her words as described some months afterwards this is what happened:

Starting in my new job in an office environment I began suffering a dull ache in my shoulder blade extending up through to my lower neck. At first I felt I must have slept awkwardly. However after six days the pain remained. Bill overheard me telling a work colleague about my discomfort and offered to help. Bill placed his hands on my shoulder for approximately five minutes and I could feel the heat in my left shoulder. Afterwards I returned to my desk, feeling slightly sceptical that the procedure had been a waste of time. However after about ten minutes my pain had disappeared and has not returned since. Thanks Bill !.

A year or so later another young lady working in another location was crouched over with pain she said which was emanating from her waist, up her side to her armpit. I tried to reassure she but she remained in pain and could not sit at her desk due to the discomfort. I told her that I had trained as a healer and said if she wished I could see what I could do to ease the pain. I didn't promise her anything but as she was so desperate she agreed. The men in the open plan office thought it was hilarious and started to make fun of my offer. I sat her in a chair as far away from the doubters as possible and applied my healing approach around her head and shoulders.

It lasted less than ten minutes and I felt drained but she walked away with a smile on her face saying she was virtually pain free. She confirmed a few days later that the pain and discomfort cleared up completely that evening and she asked me to teach her how to do the healing. Again I was as surprised as she was with the results and the men in the room became lost for words. Well whether it was an actual healing as such or the placebo effect is something perhaps that experts could form opinions on. However I also tried out the healing support on others and most people said they had enjoyed the experience although miracle cures do not happen in the process. Another lady I knew who was disabled with severe back pain and discomfort asked me to do healing on her and this in her words was the result:

When Bill gave me healing from the spirit world I felt peace and contentment. As I sat on the chair I experienced the warmth coming from Bill's hands and felt that he was transmitting energy from himself to me. As I felt the warmth I experienced a lot of tiny sparkling bright colours, such as red, green, yellow and white on an inky background. Gradually I became aware of brightness, then of a white light. I felt as though I had been transported from the room where I was sitting to another place of serenity and peace that I did not want to return from. At the time Bill gave me the healing I had suffered from chronic pain for a period of eight years. For five days afterwards I did not take all my painkillers. I found I could manage on one particular type only. I normally take four different types at different times over the day. I don't sleep very much only managing about three hours at a time before the pain breaks through. Some nights I experience no sleep at all. After Bills healing I found I was able to sleep more and experience more of a quality rest. Afterwards I felt uplifted and my whole mood had improved, as I was able to deal with my everyday life better. I would

recommend that other people have healing from Bill, as I had not experienced such improvement in many years.
Tracey.

Following that experience and kind words from Tracey I on a few more occasions tried healing on a few people – all for experience and not for any fees. One man I was trying to advise was an ex drug dealer, ex prison inmate for terms taking around ten years of his life. He was a formidable person, well built, street-wise and with a great intelligence and vision, which had taken the wrong road in life resulting in his prison terms. He had turned his life around when I met him and was seeking to turn his negatives into positives, to learn from his experiences and use that knowledge to prevent young people getting into crime and drugs. He was also setting up programmes to assist ex-offenders released from prison to find accommodation, jobs and support to prevent them re-offending.

He was feted by politicians who did not have the solutions, the media who liked his persona and innovative approach. He was so confident of his vision that he was reluctant to take my free business advice on running the company services he provided. One day in his office he told me about his painful shoulder and arm. He agreed to go into a quiet room with me and he sat on a chair. I started my healing efforts and half way through the process another ex-inmate walked into the room and probably thought we were crazy. When we had finished the feedback about the healing he gave me was very positive. He said when I was healing his feet went very hot, he felt calm and nearly went asleep. He said he found it hard to swallow at one time and couldn't move although it wasn't too uncomfortable.

Right after the healing he said his pain went and he could lift his arm over his head for the first time in eighteen months. It was a surreal experience for me to practice on someone so formidable with his background clearly in and out of prison for many years. I suppose for him to experience a culture of violence for many years to experience an episode of healing with me trying to encourage light, healing and love from above was a strange situation.

On the health diagnosis aspect I still seemed to pick up details from who knows where on people's medical conditions. To-date all the people involved have had non-serious conditions and I have not asked for fees or anything except for wishing healing and peace of mind for them. I was once reading an article about a famous health spa and clinic in central London. Many famous people apparently had treatment there including allegedly the world stage wife of a famous politician. I emailed the owner to request a meeting to ascertain her interest or otherwise in spiritual healing and she invited me down. In my reply I asked her about a shoulder/neck injury of which she confirmed when I met her in London. She apparently sustained the injury after a horse riding accident. She was amazed as I was for me to pick that up from her photograph in a magazine article.

In 2010 I was attempting some healing on my wife's friend and I picked up a problem with her toe and also information relating to a legal process she was engaged in. In particular I mentioned the name *Casablanca* to her which she was amazed as his was particularly relevant in a property name relating to that legal case underway. Again where the information came from I do not know. I am sure one day I will find out though.

On another occasion I was asked to join a group of people for a free coaching course, of which I was reluctant to participate in but I was encouraged to helping a friend out make the numbers up. There was an inspiring lady there who against the odds had dealt with immense personal tragedy in her life as a young girl and also had overcome health challenges along the way. I had said to her that she should become an inspirational speaker and use her experiences to help others in life facing major challenges. She opened her heart to the group attending the workshop, which was very brave of her and spoke of a traumatic situation regarding her Mum who had passed away some years back.

After her talk to the group I spoke to her privately and mentioned initials that had came into my thoughts when she was speaking about her Mum. I told her what the initials were which I had written down to show her and she confirmed they were that of her mother. I said to her that they were a message from her Mum to say she was ok and in a good place. Hopefully it provided comfort to her. She has since gone on to appear on national television and I am sure has a good future and a worthy life mission to achieve.

As described in my book *Downing Street Species* on what future politics should be about in terms of common good aims, selfless public service and regular MP accountability to the electorate it seemed that many of my warning signals, predictions or political prophesies had became reality. How I knew aspects of futures unfolding for others was a complete mystery for me and those involved. I suppose the starting point of premonitions was for myself listening to my own inner voice. As an allegedly healthy non-smoking, slim healthy male I had prepared for my own close call with death on Friday 13th 1992. Preparations months before arranging insurances, a will and emergency contact list in my wallet. The preparation for a future worse case scenario could have not been more comprehensive then what I had put in place. With no warning signals and a robust health screening earlier that year I was, it seemed in perfect health but I was ready for that which was to test me to the limit of my life. Perhaps my life was spared and special abilities gifted as part of my life mission in seeking a better life for as many as I could.

In respect of world events and working for the many not just the few as two psychics had forecast my political intuition or whatever you may call it seemed to manifest. My contact via Cherie Blair email and opinions/proposals to 10 Downing Street during the Prime Minister Blair Government for example. If the proposals etc were actually communicated/actioned by Tony Blair they possibly could have made a great difference and would have saved countless lives. I wrote periodically over 5 years in email to Cherie Blair via 10 Downing Street, starting before the Iraq war:

........*My proposal is that he (The Prime Minister) takes the initiative/turns the situation around by flying out to Iraq and speaking directly with the dictator in search of a solution acceptable to Britain and America. If there is a small chance that this provides a solution then he should grasp the opportunity. If Saddam fails to respond then nobody can say that Tony did not, at some risk make an attempt at the 11th hour.*

Some years later it was reported that Sir Richard Branson had a plane on standby to fly Branson and Nelson Mandela to Iraq to broker a peaceful solution to avoid bloodshed – with full approval from UN Secretary Kofi Annan. However the US/UK bombing started before they could fly out. In later years Blair flew out to Libya and embraced a *sanatised* dictator Ghadaffi who also had weapons of mass destruction, supported terrorists etc. What a shame he did not fly out and negotiate the peaceful removal of Saddam years before. I am just an ordinary guy from Liverpool, but I feel passionately that we all have the right and responsibility to try to influence others in power for the greater good.

On 8th June 2003 I wrote:

..........*Perhaps when you move from Downing St you may consider a Blair/Booth Foundation to carry on the good work you are doing on a national/international level.*

After leaving Downing Street four years or so later the Blairs did indeed set up charitable organisations. However I was not impressed when it was alleged that £120,000 was the salary of one person in the charitable trust. I know that some people would say you have to pay large sums to attract the right standard of people to drive not for profit ventures, but to slot them in the top two percent of the UK income bracket would not be my policy.

14th February 2004 I wrote:

New Labour Failures to address:

..........Parliamentary accountability has been whittled away by many different methods. This needs to be recovered and confidence rebuilt.
.........Although as a Christian I support a multi-ethnic society the economic migrant issue and shambles that it is will be a major factor in bringing down this Government. ....

Well not so much as prophecies I suppose but my opinions, although Prime Minister Brown just prior to the General election 6 years later in 2010 was caught on microphone calling a 66 year old pensioner *a bigot* after she raised her concerns with him about levels of eastern European immigration into the UK.

18th February 2004 I wrote:

..........With respect I believe that the PM may leave office considered as a good PM but will if things don't change miss that wonderful opportunity he had to be considered as a great PM.

Years later I believe that public opinion backs up this statement made by me in 2004. However in the early years of New Labour I was effectively Tony Blair's *disciple* until my disillusionment set in. I once said to Cherie Blair *I would have walked over hot coals* to support Tony Blair and his aims *for the many, not the few*. So for me it was a great disappointment that his legacy was not what I and many hoped it could have been.

12th June 2005 I wrote:

.............Perhaps the Prime Minister should review Standards in the House and work towards a system whereby all MPs are paid a new rate and consultancies and acquired directorships/nepotism etc in office are forbidden ?) please see attached. (The Democracy Trust MP Code Of Conduct)

I could see the writing on the wall as I tried previously in 2001 to get every MP to endorse a citizen focussed covenant with the people. Sadly the vast majority of MPs ignored the initiative resulting in the MP expense scandal erupting in 2009.

5th March 2006 I wrote

*......... but am disappointed in the legacy the Blair years will be leaving behind. My fear for their future is that democracy has been eroding away with our hard one freedoms haemorrhaging under the new labour project.
.............*
...............More control on our freedoms, a green light for the use of torture by third parties, law making by the unelected, the weakening of the judiciary, rewards for the party contributors of
wealth and a blind eye to declining standards in public life - now much worse than under Tory rule.
.............Near to your heart perhaps - insufficient public monies into Hospices and the care of the dying yet vast sums found to fund useless 'initiatives', computer systems, ID cards etc, etc.

Well I suppose that people's opinions may polarise on the above statements. However 5 or 6 years later investigations are still underway about the UK being complicit in the alleged arrangements with other countries like Libya leading to torture of alleged terrorists. Again reports in the media quoted in excess of £26 billion wasted on failed computer systems by the Labour government. However it was good to see the scrapping of plans to introduce costly and intrusive ID cards for all UK citizens.

1st May 2006 I wrote:

....................*A few years ago I sent you the document below, (Note: The Democracy Trust MP Code Of Conduct) which only 26 (mostly Labour MPs endorsed in 2001). It still holds true now. I intend to resend to all MPs. Why genuine/credible/ethical politicians (including the PM who was sent a copy) could not endorse it I will never know.*

Three years later the MP expense scandal erupted.

27st October 2006 I wrote:

....................How is your new book/diaries progressing.....?
Cherie later published her book. However I did not get a mention of course.

9th June 2007 I wrote:

………On a macro level this world is not a safer place, nor a more democratic place with Blairism but on the contrary the Blair Legacy leaves us all with more fears, more concerns and less freedom than in May 1997. Your heart must concur with me even though your logic may rush to defend the outcomes of the last decade. A successful economy founded on a Tory economic base saw many more billions spent, but badly invested on public services. A feel good factor by the many not a counter-balance to the mismanagement by Government of' initiatives, which have ended in waste and doubtful outcomes, nationally and globally.

The economic mess and massive debt left three years and more later as a legacy for families and their children and future generations could have been averted or minimised but Westminster was not for turning.

26th June 2007 I wrote:

………………I have, however enjoyed my visits to Downing Street etc and experiencing the historic Blair journey since 1995 through the valleys and over high mountains, and stormy weather and rainbows as it were. I do hope the new chapters in your life/Blair Foundation etc are written for the good of many and not for the few.

By a strange coincidence that evening, on the day my email headed *The Real Cherie* was sent to Cherie it was announced that a programme featuring the Prime Minister's wife was to be shown the following Wednesday night. Its title was *The Real Cherie*. (Also by another strange co-incidence my mention of rainbow in my last email was to be somewhat prophetic as a rainbow appeared over Tony Blair's constituency during the Blair's farewell visit, much to the amusement of the assembled media).

Extracts from email sent to then Shadow Home Secretary following meeting with him:

27th March 2009 I wrote:

The electorate/the country is looking for politicians to live in the real world and conduct their lives subject to selfless not selfish standards. Will Cameron, Chris Grayling and colleagues have the drive and courage to take actions to reform political standards to meet the needs of all the people ? ....Self interest is a hollow, short term high. Politics should be about making a positive difference in people's lives that are served. Too many politicians from all parties put self - interest first. David Cameron may engage with a hung Parliament next election, he may make a good Prime Minister. If he immediately reforms the greed and sleaze simmering on for a decade or more in Parliament he will go on..........

Well I suppose it wasn't too much of a prophesy but David Cameron did later become Prime Minister over a hung Parliament.

8

JUST A LITTLE PRICK

I was to hear those four piercing words countless times, both by private health and NHS care professionals on my journey of medical challenges starting from Friday 13th November 1992.. From finding a suitable vein in carrying out blood tests, to injecting me with a sedative or anaesthetic before surgical operations and procedures. The *little prick* description by the clinician was their favourite choice of words. It's a good job I didn't take their expression too seriously though. I lost count of the number of operations/invasive procedures I experienced over those years but it was around about thirty or so with me dicing with death about eight times or so in the process. I document these experiences as a record of the challenges to overcome in life's journey. Battered and bruised in many ways I always believed that life was a testing ground on how we deal with things. In my case perhaps minor challenges in the scheme of life's tragedies compared to the many medical traumas and disabilities a lot of good people have to deal with.

I had always tried to remain positive in my life and to face medical challenges as they arose but when it was two steps forward one step back over a 20 year period or so it does take its toll on your mind, body and spirit. I often looked around and constantly saw people worse off than me when the *feeling sorry for myself* shadow loomed above. Brave people, young and old dealing with severe disabilities, some recent, some lifelong inspired me and helped me put things into perspective. However as we are all human the dark challenges, the pain, the morning, afternoon and night pain or anxiety would often visit as dark clouds blotting out the light. What was interesting was that my identical twin brother had his own medical moments and challenges but not on the scale as I did. Lucky bastard I thought, well not really.

On many occasions I was a fraud, an actor who often was feeling the pain inside, the discomfort, the gloom but managed to put on a sun kissed approach to those around me. I always looked well people would say and that indeed was the case. Reasonably slim, a healthy sheen to my face, a dimpled smile to the world the illness demons inside were kept locked in, although striving to emerge to spread their wings of worry and sleepless times. The number of inpatient stays and outpatient appointment/procedures over the period since my heart attack did however give me a great perspective as a patient of both private and NHS care. As a one-time management consultant to the NHS I had been involved in many research and development projects over the years. That covered virtually every service/clinical department in hospital care including a project with the ambulance services. I covered specialisms/services such as a maternity hospital, A&E dept, mortuary/pathology services, neurosciences, outpatient clinics, total hospital re-organisation/computer systems development, medical records and I did contract consultancy work in one of the largest children's hospitals in Europe. The difference being a patient was a rude awakening in more ways than one. Some years before my wife and family used to do *mystery* guest/shopper type work for my brother Tom's business consultancy. We had to stay in some quite luxurious hotels with swimming pools as a family and record the whole customer *journey.* This was in the form of a feedback report to the client, which highlighted strengths and weaknesses of the hotel services. The client with my brother's help would then focus the training and development resource on the gaps in service. It was great for us as it provided many free breaks when the children were young. The spin-off from those experiences was that during my medical episodes when I had quiet, symptom free moments I was always evaluating the medical and housekeeping services whilst under medical care. Even my wife would be checking the availability of soap and towels, the quality of bedding, meal services etc when she came to visit me. She had much higher standards than I did however.

The reality of being a patient and relying on others to attend to care and personal needs was much different than swanning around the hospitals with my best business suit on and trying to think of intelligent questions to ask with initiatives to implement thus justifying my consultancy fees. To feel the pain certainly gives you a perspective on the needs of others and the realities of healthcare. The starting point for me was clearly my massive heart attack on that luck Friday 13th when I survived. Although with a brave face I left the hospital a nervous wreck I shuddered when the sirens of an ambulance close by triggered off a nervous reminder of that traumatic day. I invested in a mobile phone then, which were just coming into fashion or as a business necessity. It accompanied me and gave comfort if I was on my own. I always carried aspirin with me as an emergency blood thinning aid if I felt the heart problem coming on. I arranged for my wife and step-daughters to receive first aid training in dealing with a heart attack, which gave me some comfort.

They got a certificate and I got peace of mind. It was always difficult for me to assess my cardiac status as I was also diagnosed with a hiatus hernia, which gave me almost immediate pain, discomfort etc in the centre of my chest when walking even a short distance. Was it angina, was it the hiatus hernia has always been a dilemma to deal with. Shortness of breath and a periodic but long term painful foot problem on walking was a problem also.

On being discharged from the hospital following my cardiac arrest that November I went to see a GP at my doctor's surgery. The doctor was a very relaxed person and suggested that I just take it easy and stay off work for about six months. No investigations were advised and I left the surgery somewhat unsettled. It was only a few weeks after the heart attack and I was still very nervous to say the least of every twinge in my body. Was it indigestion I felt or was it cardiac related pain was my quandary. Luckily I, at great expense had insured for private health care provision years back when I went self-employed and I sought a specialist opinion. I contacted a cardiologist who had an outstanding professional reputation whom my elder brother Jim was seeing and tests were soon arranged.

I subsequently had an angiogram, which is an x ray of the heart after a wire and a dye had entered the heart arteries to facilitate the x ray views. An overhead x ray machine produced an image of the beating heart and blood flow through the arteries. I was informed that the main (left anterior descending) artery was more than 98% blocked and that remedial action was necessary. I was told I needed an angioplasty, which involved the wire catheter being inserted in an artery in my groin area and up to inside my heart. The procedure was in an operating theatre, without anaesthetic and was pretty scary. It started with *just a little prick incision* by the doctor in the groin artery to insert the catheter and inject the dye into the heart arteries.

The catheter wire was introduced with a deflated balloon into the blockage area and the balloon inflated to effectively compress the obstruction to allow a greater blood flow. This was the angioplasty element of the procedure. The whole process I found rather scary although the pain and discomfort was minimal. The fact that a wire is in the centre of your heart would stimulate the imagination of any patient as to what could happen during the procedure. In the background pop music was playing as per the choice of the cardiologist in charge. I don't think that the song *spirit in the sky* would have been my choice though. Perhaps the song *aint no stopping me now* or something similar would have been more appropriate. After the procedure the doctor had to hold his thumb over the entry wound after the wire was removed. This can last for ten minutes or more so that the wound can clot and prevent heavy blood loss. I recall him on one occasion taking his thumb away for a second or so and the blood spurting as a mini fountain onto his white overall.

I went on to have about ten angiograms over the years with seven memorable occasions when my artery blocked up again resulting in life affecting symptoms and concern for me and my family. On one occasion whilst the procedure was underway a nurse went over to open a defibrillator case, which was the device to restart the heart after a heart attack. Watching her from the operating trolley was frightening, but it obviously turned out to be not relevant to me on that day. It nearly caused me to have a heart attack though with my fears held within. I did ask the cardiologist about my residual heart damage on another occasion and he told me that nearly a third of my heart muscle was dead after my cardiac arrest experience. Quite a sobering thought indeed and something to live with over the years. I mentioned to one of the GPs at my doctors practice about the cardiologist diagnosis from the heart scans and the accompanying *left ventricular dysfunction* description. The GP with a straight face said oh that is something that *eventually leads to complete heart failure* or words to that effect. I thought well, that was reassuring for me to look forward to. I wondered whether that particular GP had registered with the heart organ donation register for such an eventuality in the community.

Further down my medical episode trail I discovered a dry funny shaped pimple along my hairline by my ear, which I showed to my GP. A quick referral to a specialist resulted in me again lying on an operating table whilst a cheery private health funded surgeon removing the unwanted pimple. On discharge that day when I asked the surgeon what the condition was he quite cheerfully informed me it was a *rodent ulcer*. To me it sounded like something that rats got, which in my case (in the opinion of some) was quite appropriate to me. Ex love-rat etc, etc. On return home I hot-footed it to my computer to do an internet search of the surgical diagnosis. It seemed that the rodent ulcer description was another name for *basal skin carcinoma.* Shit, skin cancer it said and that was the bad news I had to deal with. Again thoughts of my mortality were going through my mind and this new setback to delivering my life mission. However the good news was it was easily treatable if caught early before it became too invasive and spread - often with grim results.

The photographs on the web of the advanced condition were enough to put anybody off their breakfast and out of the suns harmful rays for a lifetime. I had another suspicious sun damaged pimple removed from my chest area a few years later. Probably a legacy from my youthful days lying in the sun on Spanish beaches, no sun tan oil applied with a beer or *cuba libre* in my hand watching the girls go by and listening to pop music. As it turned out ten years on the offending bits have not returned so fingers crossed. Another bridge crossed, another small mountain climbed.

A few years after my heart attack I started to get pains in my stomach and some blood loss from the back end, which caused me some obvious concern. I saw the cheery pimple-removing surgeon who coincidently I used to bump into in a local traditional pub called the *Freshfield.* I did make a mental note that he always seemed to be drinking non-alcoholic drinks at the bar, which really impressed me. A surgeon with a hangover was not my cup of tea. The surgeon sent me off to a Liverpool hospital to have a nuclear scan as he described it to obtain confirmation about his diagnosis. He was spot on with his theory and the scan result was that I had a very rare condition called *meckels diverticulum*, which was present from birth. It sounded a bit gory but basically a small sac, like a mini-stomach was attached to my intestine. This was prone to bleeding, ulceration and could cause life-threatening complications. From what I can remember I think the decision was to monitor the condition. The pain etc came and went until one day I started bleeding profusely and felt most unwell. I phoned a medical help-line and the doctor suggested I take iron tablets, which knowing the pain and symptoms I was having was just inappropriate advice to me the patient in great need. That night it got worse and the blood loss was terrific and my wife called out the on-call GP. She took one look at the substantial collection of blood and called an ambulance.

On emergency admission to A & E I felt very ill and whilst awaiting treatment I really believed I was dying and wondering whether my heart would take it. At one point I started to drift off and felt my life and spirit ebbing away to another place. My wife and the nurse caring for me looked very panicky and I felt like my time was up at that stage. Apparently I had lost a lot of blood and I could feel the effects. I underwent major surgery with a chunk of my insides removed and was left with a large vertical scar through my tummy button to my groin. The following ten days spent in hospital were probably the worst experience in my life with me feeling extremely unwell. I did not have the strength even to talk to my wife or visitors and the pain was very bad. I prayed hard for relief over those ten days and things slowly got back to near normal. It was very embarrassing as nurses had to take me to the toilet and I had to relearn how to take food and go the toilet again with the dedicated nursing staff. They cleaned and encouraged me as I was quite helpless much of the time then. The indignity was awful for me a 40 something male, who could not look after himself.

In the end I got through the major surgery and after effects, albeit not in one piece but equipped enough to face many more challenges. I found out later that George Washington had apparently had the same condition but in those days of course they did not have x ray machines. My usual surgeon was not around to perform the emergency surgery and when I saw him afterwards he said he was disappointed he didn't carry out that operation as he had only came across a few cases of the condition during his professional life. I wondered how my genetically identical twin brother did not get the same condition as well as all the other ailments targeted me over the previous years and beyond.

The resultant surgical scar became a blessing in disguise a week or so later and saved our family a lot of money when that poor tax collector caught sight of my *war wounds*. The lasting legacy of the *meckels* surgery was a weakened area around my stomach. I developed internal scar tissue – called adhesions, which often happens after such surgery and these were to bring excruciating painful spasms, sickness and discomfort over the years. I tried to fight the pain when I could, which mostly hit me after an evening meal but often I was in agony and an ambulance was called or I was driven by car to A&E. I lost count of the number of times I was admitted as an emergency and given morphine for that condition. Around 2004 I had major surgery to attempt to sort out the adhesions in a private hospital. When I came around after the surgery I was in agony and being very sick, which just aggravated the wound site and stitches. I did not feel like drinking or eating and the doctor seemed quite patronising treating me as if I had a toothache. I knew something was not right. Again I felt dreadful and was in a weakened state frequently going the toilet and also being violently ill. Eventually I was diagnosed with an infection and I lost a stone in weight and did not feel well for a year or so afterwards. Whether I acquired the infection in the private hospital I probably will never know. It was some coincidence that the symptoms started right after the surgery.

The operation did not resolve the adhesion problem and to this day I still experience periodic severe pain and feeling unwell. Those symptoms were to end up with me having numerous *oscopys* etc of the intrusive kind over the years both down my mouth into my stomach etc and from another embarrassing direction. Most of the intrusive procedures I had had were in private hospitals and under sedation. In a few situations under NHS care I was given the procedure without sedation. With one prolonged investigation the clinician who was a female seemed to be using a mop handle or other such blunt instrument and the pain had me a so called brave male crying out. She kept saying *nearly done, your doing well* and other such words of comfort for me but I thought she was a pain in the proverbial ass if you will excuse the pun. I expected the mop handle to appear out of my mouth or nose at one point but I survived to fight another day. To be fair what I did notice over the 20 or so years of serial patient episodes was that the quality of NHS care was rapidly getting better and the care provided by the private healthcare sector was getting worse. The year on increases in the private health care premiums for my family became unaffordable anyway and I cancelled the policy with my growing confidence in the NHS. The NHS started using private hospitals anyway and I ended up as a NHS patient at a private hospital locally. I ended up seeing the same Consultant who actually treated me privately some years before for an ENT condition. The waiting time was only a couple of weeks and it was good to reminisce and swop jokes with the affable specialist.

Along the way I suffered from severe hay fever type symptoms, muzzy head, fatigue etc, which turned out to be nasal polyps. Minor problems in the scheme of things but a proverbial pain in the butt on top of everything else. I had one operation by an ENT specialist to remove polyps and a nasal spur whatever that was. A few years later the symptoms had returned and I saw another ENT specialist who said I needed another operation to resolve the polyps and infected sinuses. Coincidently I picked up some psychic type stuff about his family and son in particular and told the specialist about his son's non-life threatening problem affecting his walking at that time. He was quite impressed and I was again surprised to again be reminded of the occasional remote view medical diagnosis gift I had. It was arranged that I went into a private hospital for the operation.

On arrival they asked for my credit card details. I suppose they were protecting their cash flows if the patients expired in their care. A nurse came to take my blood and said it would be *just a jab,* which was a new term to me. She said that one guy in the hospital actually took offence when she mentioned the *little prick* expression. When my wife and I got settled into the hospital the private healthcare luxury we were expecting just did not exist. The room was dismal and badly furnished. When I was wheeled up to the operating theatre the pre-op room was little more than a storeroom full of clutter akin to a teenager's bedroom.

The surgeon explained the risks and said that as he was operating through the nose close to the brain there was always a possibility of some damage to the brain lining. I thought *shit, I'am not a celebrity – get me out of here.* The operation went ahead that night and I was taken back to my hut of a room and felt quite ill. I had trouble breathing and told the nurses that I did not feel very well and had symptoms were similar to way I felt before my heart attack. Sometimes whilst lying in my bed in the different hospitals I kept a rough and ready journal of what I was feeling and what was happening around me. Referring back to my own diary notes some two years later I had written *After op – couldn't breathe, pins in arms, hard to lift legs and arms, bleeding clots from nose.* I think by then the surgeon had gone home to watch TV or something and I could not get the nurses to take my condition seriously. I asked for the telephone and phoned my wife. She spoke to the nurses and asked them to satisfy my request to place an ECG, heart monitor on my chest. They spent about half an hour looking for one and came back with a contraption looking like equipment from a *back to the future* film. It didn't seem to work and I got more and more anxious. Eventually around midnight my wife and the surgeon arrived and he tried to reassure me that it was a panic attack and that I was hyperventilating. He said there was cocaine in the treatment and that kicks in after two hours.

As a veteran of many, many operations I knew that a panic attack was not the case. I subsequently recovered and went home with a bloodied nose. I shortly afterwards decided to revisit my cardiologist and had an angiogram in the operating theatre. The nature of my condition was hard to ascertain but after detailed scrutiny of the heart arteries and x rays from many different angles the doctor told me that the main artery was indeed severely blocked – again over 95%. The post-operative symptoms after my previous operation were indeed real, not imagined and I was probably very lucky to survive that operation considering the state of my heart. The cardiologist inserted a stent tube into the main artery and saved my life once again. Thank goodness for warm hearted, extremely competent Dr David Ramsdale from Liverpool who certainly knew his chosen specialism and delivered care with such a warm heart and modest manner. I remember asking him did he not think of the ripple effect of his life saving care. He had saved so many lives and enriched the lives of the family and friends of those patients who faced death but were given another chance by him and his team. His reply again was modest and unassuming.

Three years afterwards looking as fit as the proverbial fiddle I was feeling unwell and although

157

initial medical opinion did not seem concerned I asked to be referred back to Dr Ramsdale. I went into hospital on my birthday and had an exploratory procedure in the cardiac operating theatre. It was surreal as I was scared but joking with the operating theatre staff and next minute they all gathered around my trolley and sang happy birthday to me. I was very embarrassed but touched by their kindness. My birthday *present* half an hour later in theatre was to be told by Dr Ramsdale that my other main coronary artery was more than 95% blocked. It couldn't be done that day as they had to put me on blood thinning drugs for a month before the operation.

Happy bloody birthday I thought. I was wheeled back to the recovery ward and had to remain still for hours, which was most uncomfortable but the nursing staff and entertaining catering lady were fantastic. She was always telling jokes and being quite flirty. Sadly though she told me she had a twin brother who had died when quite young. Whilst staring at the ceiling about seven nursing staff gathered around my bedside a birthday cake appeared and again they all started singing happy birthday. Surreal again but warm and comforting to me at my hour of need.

I had tears in my eye when I thanked them for their kindness. I left their care that day to face a month of concern awaiting my operation whilst thinking my artery would block completely. The following operation was a success however my heart did not feel the same as it seemed to have episodes of rapid heart beats at rest and I was always exhausted. My daughter Lucy had recently flown out to Dubai to take up a new job travelling the world and I had kept secret my operation so not to worry her.

I also developed many hernias after repeat abdominal surgery and lost count after about five or so remedial operations. Most hernias except one were painful prior to the operations and affected my life-style over those years. I tried to grin and bear the pain and discomfort but on each occasion ended up with surgery. The problem being that each operation presented future potential problems and some related risks and long-term consequences as I discovered. After one of the alleged straight-forward hernia operations, yet again in a private hospital I developed what is called a haematoma. This is a blood loss, which in my case presented itself as severe internal bruising from above my stomach down to my now swollen testicles. In case of complications I asked my wife to photograph the condition and the vivid red, black and blue colours and effects looked like something from a horror film. A few years later the film was still not developed and my wife took about a dozen rolls of film to be developed locally. We had forgotten that roll amongst the others and my wife's embarrassment on collecting the photographs was clear to see. I wondered if copies had been made to appear on *facebook* one day to embarrass me at a time not so distant.

After that operation in March 2008 and before my post-operative complication took hold I did an impromptu psychic reading on a couple of nurses who verified the psychic information I gave. At 11.00pm that night I was looking at the dressing over the operation site and it was amazing to see a small blood leakage on the dressing in the perfect shape of a heart against the white dressing background. Only problem was it was 5 weeks early for St Valentines day. The minor miracle turned sour when after discharge I experienced severe progressive swelling/blood leakage under my skin over a large area and emergency admission to NHS hospital a few days later.

Six months or so before that I had a repeat hernia on the same location and after discharge from the private hospital I began to feel unwell. Embarrassing again but just my luck again I thought. I began to feel most unwell with a severely swollen testicle. It really peed me off if you will pardon the description. Between my wife and I we phoned the private hospital on four occasions and explained the symptoms and we were given reassurance. We were told that everything was quite normal and not to worry. At no point was I asked to return to the private hospital or to seek medical advice and I consequently became even more ill. I reached a point where I nearly collapsed at home and was consequently admitted via A&E to the local NHS hospital. The infection had made me very dizzy and disorientated as well as being painful. The NHS doctor quickly diagnosed a severe infection and I was put on a drip, given antibiotics and kept in hospital for four days. In the NHS hospital September 26th 2007 I made some notes. I read it for the first time since then in August 2010. I had written:
What is the infection ?, what is the diagnosis ?, it is still painful, it is still swollen, how long will it last ?
Overnight the poor man next to me was retching all night. Not much compassion shown by the South African nurse – not prejudiced but just no emotion from her.

I sent texts to my wife and Terry the matron of the hospice we were fighting to save. I texted the words: *to feel the pain and suffering with others facing much more than I helps me to understand and takes me forward.* At 2.15pm that day I wrote: '*I feel my life is wasting in here, part of a band of elders who have seen greater years and greater ills currently. My energy seems subsumed and weakened against their ailments and advanced years. An unwelcome guest in a big brother reality ward. I feel sapped and this is a testing time. The energy of youth is not around me and I need to escape and embrace a younger life-charge. Jump leads to youthful faces and energy stores'.* I went to help a fellow patient who looked cold and uncomfortable.

He was a long stay patient with severe bowel problems following a twisted hernia. I was trying to arrange his pillows when his bowel erupted in a release of bad smells. He was very embarrassed but obviously couldn't help it. He seemed a nice guy and his wife who visited twice a day was still very devoted and loving to him, which was nice to see. At 9.25pm I had written: *I am asking God/family above for a sign whether I would have time to complete my life mission ?.* In the peaceful ward of three people I look around but nothing moves or falls. However a bang at the side of the bed was a towel falling onto the nurse pager. The Ronan Keating song came into my head with the words *you say it best when you say nothing at all.*

At 5.30pm the following day I was eating the so called hospital *dinner* when the old guy aged about 80 from the opposite bed came over. He said: when is it *going to happen ?.* He told me he was in fear of his life and it was going to *happen that night*. He accused the patient in the next bed to me of putting orange juice in his urine bottle. Said he was telling the police. He said *what sort of sticky end to you see for me, are you after my money or my body*. He said *try to make it quicker – with no blood on me*. The night shift nurse came on duty and he asked her strange questions. He said *what have you got for me* ? – she said *a big hammer*. My notes said that that *fxxxxd him completely*. Very sad as it was it was humorous but I felt guilty as he was someone's dad, husband, friend, brother etc and he could be any one of us one day.

Eventually I was allowed home to my safe haven of younger people and loving care. The private healthcare surgeon who conducted the operation made his diagnosis some weeks later. He said the infection was called *epididymo-orchitis*. He told me that the pain would ease off in weeks, but the swelling could take months to go down. It did take me months for the swelling to go down. The consequence was that I suffered permanent damage from the effects of the infection. In the words from the Beatles song *I was half the man I used to be* if you know what I mean. The swelling shrunk far too much and permanent damage was done, which was to have knock on consequences. I clearly was not satisfied with the results of my phone calls of concerns/lack of medical follow up from the private hospital. But that as they say is another story.

Reflecting on my health challenges they appeared in different forms in every one of the years since my heart attack and I was getting increasingly fed up visiting hospitals. In one hospital alone I was informed that they had around one thousand sheets of case notes in my file. From head to toe I had health issues. From the top down I underwent three surgical operations near the lining of the brain on sinus/polyp problems. I had ongoing hiatus hernia effects, periodic stomach problems and abdominal pain perhaps related to post-operative adhesions. My heart had experienced about ten or more surgical procedures and the heart muscle was 30% dead effectively. I had post-operative permanent damage effectively affecting my manhood with all the knock on effects. My soles and ankles suffered periodic severe pain often affecting my walking and sometimes painful at rest which literally stopped me in my tracks. The specialist said it was something I had to live with. I had countless invasive investigations and tests, numerous days as inpatient and outpatient in hospitals. What I have discovered along the way is that doctors are also fallible and it is essential to follow ones instincts and proactively seek the appropriate medical care you think you need. Also somebody once said to me that *heaven is full of people who did not want to bother doctors.* That statement is so valid and worth considering.

Apart from all that I am lucky to be alive and compared with others who have far greater challenges I count myself lucky still to be here and making ripples in this world. I have met many psychics and healers in my time and they all seem to have had or are experiencing health challenges in their lives. Perhaps that is the price to pay for the gifts they have and to feel the pain is to be able to understand more the needs of others who are suffering so that they can be helped. However Archbishop Desmond Tutu was reported to have said to God above that he had had enough tests and challenges in his life's journey of faith and did not want any more challenges. I understand his sentiments entirely. The path of life is weary but the negatives can be turned into positives with the dark clouds of despair making way for sunshine, beautiful sunsets, bright rainbows and sparkling stars eternal.

9

LAST CHAPTER

It is estimated that some two thirds of people believe in the paranormal and experience in different degrees this mysterious aspect of life. Many people have intuitive experiences such as that thinking of someone when that person calls by telephone or turns up unexpected. My experiences are not earth shattering but perhaps worth considering by those interested in unexplained psychic happenings. Events witnessed by many with the absence of any logical or scientific explanation as to where the information comes from and how on random occasions I can see events and precise details locked away in people's minds or hidden from view. Some events presented to me but yet to happen in the future. However, some may offer well thought out reasons to explain the experiences away or disbelieve completely. Indeed some may say I am crazy or have imagined the events and that is a challenge I can live with.

I can understand the sceptics and respect their views on something they cannot disprove or prove but I cannot rewrite history to fit my life into what is considered the norm. I am confident I have sufficient independent witnesses to verify many of these events including credible people who can validate the authenticity of the various situations. I can only be what I am, as a person touched by these events, touching others with these events and other life situations. Combined it contributes to who I am. I believe what I believe within the framework of Christian beliefs and can only relate the events as they actually happened.

It seems I am in good company and perhaps also in bad company regarding psychic beliefs. Apparently during the war years Sir Winston Churchill consulted a clairvoyant named Richard Hickland and in later years he consulted an American psychic named Shirley Carson. Documents held in UK national archives suggest that during the second-world war the UK intelligence services actually recruited a cross-dressing psychic, Louis de Wohl to read Adolf Hitler's star signs. Hitler had apparently a policy not to make strategic decisions before consulting his horoscope prepared by German Astrologer – Karl Krafft. You couldn't make it up I suppose. I wonder if the Astrologer later went into cheese production as an alternative career. It seemed that he with Hitler could not predict Hitlers sticky end in Berlin. In my working life I have been viewed as a practical person and allegedly down to earth. By career an engineer, an advisor to companies, charities, politicians and individuals and have operated with a no nonsense approach to life. I consider myself driven by fact, by evidence and what I can see and feel with my own eyes and senses.

However I can only say that when faced with unexplained events such as I and others have experienced, I believe that mysterious forces are definitely at work. I think it is important that we all should have an open mind and not reject the things we cannot understand. I am certain that the forces that come into play are not of evil intent but believe they are part of the myriad of seen and unseen energies of this world and beyond. Perhaps all the questions we have about such forces and phenomena will be answered one day. I have never found my experiences scary in the least and feel, for want of a better description somewhat privileged for such episodes being included in my normal life. Such happenings only firm up my belief that we are all here for a purpose in life, that perhaps we are judged on what we do with our lives and that our spirit and souls do move on when our earthly journey is completed here. I am absolutely confident that I will meet mam and dad and other loved ones when we pass on and that I am not afraid to make that journey, hopefully with God's love around to help me and others that follow. Those people blessed with special gifts, abilities and powers carry with them a responsibility not to be abused and surely must use the ability for the common good and not solely for personal gain.

Life is a mixture of light and dark, good and bad, love and hate. The paths that people take in life are in many ways affected by circumstances but free choice on how we relate to other people is given. I generalise people into givers and takers and very often we meet people who are in both categories. I have met some great role models in my life but also many people I describe as losing their soul along the way. My heroes include a friend Martin who developed multiple sclerosis and carried on working without complaint and supporting his family until his untimely death. Another hero is Lawrence Paton who totally blind set up a charity in my hometown to help blind and partially sighted people. I saw an article about him setting up a day centre and went to meet him and offer support. He was on his knees scraping old carpet from the floor when I went in. Another fantastic person was a youngish guy who without wages was running a youth centre in a poor area of Hackney in London. I saw him on the *secret millionaire* TV programme and went down to meet him and later obtained an invite for him to 10 Downing Street. On the day of visiting Downing Street he was suffering badly with the effects of treatment for his cancer condition but he was glad he made it on the day.

With me that day also at No 10 was Rob Lloyd a tireless support to all he met and in particular the free professional support over the years to a Liverpool based hospice charity. On the down side of life we meet many people who I would describe as *selling their souls* along the way to make money, achieve power or just put their selfish needs first. We have all met them I presume. Those I recall who promise much, who take without giving, who say they will do things but don't deliver or abandon principles and integrity for short or long term gain disappoint me and I have met many like that along the way. I started writing a short story one day, yet unfinished called *Give or take a lifetime*. In it I present a scenario where the scene is an elderly person sitting by a fireplace in the last period of their life. The question they ponder is what legacy are they leaving behind in terms of love, selflessness, generosity and what is the warmth that other people do and feel for them. They might look around at their assets and if appropriate to ask was it all worth it and were the material comforts achieved with integrity ? Was there a price worth paying and have I been a giver or a taker in life ? is another question to consider in that armchair setting. The ripple effect of their actions in their lives should as measured by good not bad outcomes and be a form of comfort not regret at that time of life. The worldly goods will remain or gather dust but the impact of that person on others along life's journey will live on in spirit and in people's hearts eternal.

There is a flower power hippie type pop song in my head from decades ago, which lyrics include the words *we are stardust*, which may have some credence when you stop and think about it. We on earth perhaps originated from energy forms billions of years ago as particles of the stars and the galaxies originating from a place God created. Mankind formed in a beginning beyond our comprehension of time, distance and space. The cosmic dust and debris from stars providing the basis for our existence lost in time emerging with tireless evolution. Stardust perhaps blended with a soul, a spirit force that can neither be created nor destroyed by mortal means. Many months after first writing the above comments about *cosmic dust and debris from stars providing the basis for our existence.* I spotted an article in various newspapers and on TV about dust recently collected in space by a space-probe from the tail of a comet. It seems that scientists seemed to have discovered some evidence of the building blocks of life in the dust from the comet.

It follows that the songwriter was correct and yet again a strange co-incidence occurred yet again when I re-presented that theory in my writing and the issue was to emerge in the media shortly afterwards. In my case I can but wonder why I have experienced the strange events that I have and speculate what comes next on this planet in the time as short as it is or as long as it is. What lies beyond this world is something else, but holds no fear for me and can only be another place to call home, to find peace. A place where we all ultimately reunite, evaluate the journey and gain answers to this stage of our cycle as mortals, spirits or souls as God decides. Of course our view of what heaven is like and the reality when we move on is speculation to us all. Faith is what takes us forward and for those who have no faith in a heaven or a better place to pass over to then their only reassurance is total oblivion. Silence awaiting them with no pain, no hunger, no love, no hate, and no sunrises or sunsets.

My faith supports me, albeit a mortal spirit who is more of a sinner than a saintly man, not really a churchgoer, more an idealist seeking to right wrongs. Passionate and determined to explore the boundaries of our existence in search of a better life for myself and others. An explorer of life as short or as long as it may be conscious of the expression, *no pain – no gain* in our life's mission. The life mission continues, much yet to experience, more challenges to arise with psychic events still blossoming to flavour lives. Death, when it visits will be a natural change holding no fears as life events have strengthened my spirit. We are all spirits here on earth and our spirits live on. With those thoughts in mind I had on many occasions written goodbye letters to my family and friends just in case with the aim of giving them comfort and presenting my faith in afterlife and meeting up again in a place of love with our loved ones. My just in case goodbye notes covered most of my challenging years of serious illness from the 1992 near death heart attack. In 2004 I wrote two letters when dealing with more surgery etc.

On 14th March 2007 I wrote: *To all that I love I will love you forever. Do not weep, I only sleep and we will all meet again. Fear not, love is endless and our love goes on. I hear your whisper, I see your tears, do not despair you will find peace.* On 23rd July 2007 at 11-48pm, whilst in hospital I wrote again: *I lie here again in my hospital bed nearing midnight and put my life's thoughts down. Yet again my mortality is challenged. To all that I love, my friendships enduring, to many others giving less, expecting much I thank you all for being yourselves. The tapestry of life must have that balance of the good, the bad even to mould our life's work and everlasting soul.*

Our soul, which lives on. Life is part of our existence, which never dies and we with our spirit, are as indestructible as stardust, which gave us our life. A gift from a greater being, all to be revealed one day in another place. We are judged by others here not having the qualities to judge us. Judged also by unknown forces, which we will blend with one day. A day that shall not be called a day because eternity will replace days. With time not experienced, without the ticking clock. A place called home bathed in love. On this world of joy and pain we are born with the opportunity of decision making, paths which selected can impact on many. As a pebble in a pond the ripple effect of our lives can and does impact on many. We all have a life mission but are oblivious to its purpose.

No matter what faith we have or don't have we all have a responsibility to try to make a positive difference or contribution to the lives of others. Many cast the pebble in the pond, turn their backs and walk away. Those that I have loved in many different ways have inspired me, motivated me and have enriched my life. Enriched and motivated by family and friends in so many ways. My writing was interrupted by a patient much older than me who came over to my bedside. He said his father died a young 41 year old, his brother died at 28, a friend broke his neck in an accident, his first and then second wife died and that someone else got knocked down by a bus. He ended up by saying, *well I've had a good life.* You just couldn't make it up I thought and he wasn't joking as he was quite serious.

On 26th September 2007 lying in bed in ward 15B of Southport General Hospital I had written the following (unedited) thoughts into words. It wasn't Shakespeare but it was from the heart:

To all that I hold close and love, from the babies to much older. My friends, my extended family and those I have worked with, spent time with and respected in my lifetime this is my message. As always with me a message from my heart, supported by my mind and everlasting in my spirit and soul.

I wish to go on to do so much for others in this world and my fear is that my life mission is cut short before I achieve my goals. Death has no fear as we are all part of Gods family and we will go on and onwards like stardust. We are energy and cannot be destroyed. My sadness is the sadness on earth that moving on to join other loved ones will produce to you all. Do not be sad too long as I am with you as long as the stars last in the skies above us. My comfort in life has been unseen loved ones, my father, my mother and others who have taken steps by my side in my life's journey and in my minds eye. Feel my love around you as I will be there. Grief is a natural process and the pain you feel will ease with time has it did with me when my faith in everlasting life grew as the years went on. Feel no guilt when sometimes I am not in your thoughts and life is good for you. I will know. We are here to be judged to make a positive difference in the lives of others. We are human, we fail often.

My message is to be positive, give rather than take, develop high principles and move on. Learn from the many sins we carry out and are tested with. Be generous with others, material gains in your life can be hollow comforts if you lose or sell your soul along the way. Selfless rather than selfish will bring much greater rewards along the way. Do not weep or feel the pain too long as you have your own life mission to finish after mine has gone. Close your eyes and I will be there. The rustle of the leaves in the trees, the drop of a feather at your feet, the beauty of the sky at night, the sunset will be shared equally. Speak and I will listen and share. The dark of the night will always be followed by sunrise and another day to move forward with hope, love and life. I and others who love you will be close to you. William, your husband, Dad, Brother, friend, brother in law, uncle, grandfather, dads baba and soulmate. Love you forever xx (xxx)

On 14th March 2008 whilst in hospital again I also wrote the following: *To all that I love, you are all that I love. Our love (and friendship) will last as long as the stars shine in the sky. We will all be together one day in the place of great love with others gone before whose place in our hearts and soul is eternal. We should have no fear of what life brings us nor be afraid of what after-life sets out for us. Love is eternal and like energy cannot be destroyed. Our life mission is to love and give and in the process if we suffer than so be it as the reasons will be clear one day. Love you forever x (xxxx).*

The message I wanted to send out clearly was that I did not want to move on from this life but that if I did then the passing away was yet another chapter in our existence. I had a powerful faith in God above, around and within us and the reunion of souls and spirits. I had seen so many unexplained things in my life like the prophesies, like the messages and information about others passed on that could only come from another place. Many like me are perhaps child-like in some ways when things get tough and we speak or send thoughts or pleas for help and support from our parents who have passed on or to other loved ones in that place of rest. As a grandfather myself now silent prayers to mam and dad just don't seem logical but love lives on and they hear those words. When remembered a *good night* spoken or thought sent to those loved ones above is not wasted as they will hear.

My concern of life's end in this world was always for the grief left behind, but that is another test in life that we all face and how we deal with it is what matters. Saying goodbye to this life is followed by a welcome hello in the following life. Such is life as they say, onwards and upwards hopefully with this life's mission over. Over apart from the legacy of actions, outcomes, achievements and for many a gene pool to carry on where we left off. Having faith is the key, giving and sharing love opens the doors for experiences that dreams are made of.

Lightning Source UK Ltd.
Milton Keynes UK
UKOW051007220612

194856UK00001B/11/P